THE WORLDLY
EVANGELICALS

THE WORLDLY EVANGELICALS

Richard Quebedeaux

1817

Published in San Francisco by

HARPER & ROW, PUBLISHERS

New York, Hagerstown, San Francisco, London

1. Evangelicalism — United States

Grateful acknowledgment is made to *Radical Religion,* Berkeley, CA, for permission to reprint "A Rediscovery of the Christian Faith" by Edith Black (Winter 1973). © 1973 Radical Religion Collective.

Grateful acknowledgment is also made to *Christianity and Crisis,* New York, New York, for permission to quote from "The Evangelicals: New Trends and New Tensions," 36, No. 14 (September 20 1976). © 1976 *Christianity and Crisis.*

FIRST EDITION

Designed by Jim Mennick

Library of Congress Cataloging in Publication Data

Quebedeaux, Richard.
   THE WORLDLY EVANGELICALS.

   Includes bibliographical references and index.
   1. Evangelicalism—United States. I. Title.
BR1642.U5Q4   1978   270.8'2   77-7841
ISBN 0-06-061380-7

---

78 79 80 81 82 10 9 8 7 6 5 4 3 2 1

For Bruce Taylor and Ina J. Kau
with warm affection

You know well enough, Man, what is good!
For what does the Lord require from you,
But to be just, to love mercy,
And to walk humbly with your God?

Micah 6:8
(J. B. Phillips, *Four Prophets*)

Contents

Preface

It was Bob Dylan who said, "He not busy bein' born is busy dying." In the course of just the last few years, *born again*—the once laugh-provoking term describing evangelical Christians—has become a respectable, if not glamorous, designation, no less fashionable and chic than the growing number of national celebrities who unabashedly declare that they have been born again. Evangelical Christianity has finally emerged from its anticultural ghetto into the mainstream of American life. It is now a force to be reckoned with.

Much has happened since June 1973, when I delivered the manuscript of my first book to its publisher. *The Young Evangelicals,* the title of that work, has also come to signify a new religious consciousness, a new generation of evangelical Christians who repudiate and disown the social and political conservatism and culture rejection of traditional evangelicalism without giving up the basic tenets and faith of Christian orthodoxy. These generally younger Christians of the evangelical left are now fully acceptable in the wider society, even within the liberal religious and secular academic and activist communities; while modern evangelicals of the right and center, flaunting their ever increasing upward social mobility, are also hailed in big business, sports, Washington politics, and the mass media. In *The Young Evangelicals,* I predicted that the mainline Protestant liberal establishment ("mainstream ecumenical liberalism") would shortly yield its preeminence in middle-class, white American society to evangelicalism as the new mainline expression of Christianity,

shared by Catholics as well as Protestants. Today, mainstream evangelicalism has already become a reality.

One purpose of the present work is to help secular and nonevangelical
religious readers understand the evangelicals—who they are, what they
believe, how they behave, and where they are changing. But I have also
written for the evangelicals themselves, to assist them in discerning
exactly where they are now, where they're going, and whether that's
really where they want to end up. In this connection many evangelicals
will not like what I say or the way I say it. True, the present work is not a
presentation and interpretation of scientifically gathered research data
(though a bit *is* included). Neither do I wish to speak for anyone but
myself; I describe trends and tensions merely as I see them. Nevertheless,
I have good reason to believe that my analysis, though sketchy and
tentative, is essentially correct; and I urge my evangelical critics to consider what I've said carefully before accusing me of falsehood.

Those who have already read *The Young Evangelicals*—still a very
useful essay dealing with historical and sociological background material
omitted in the present work—will note that I am not quite as optimistic
and uncritical in treating the evangelical left as I was five years ago. At
that time I assumed that evangelicals could be genuinely faithful to the
Gospel (and "progressive") only insofar as they became more like—but
not too much like—liberals. However, now that this liberalizing tendency among evangelicals is readily apparent and growing, I'm no longer
certain that it's a good thing at all. To my mind the Christian faith at its
core is no more a liberal stance than it is a conservative position. Rather,
it is inherently *radical,* as anyone who takes it seriously—who makes his
or her life "a living sacrifice" (Romans 12:1)—will surely find out.

I would like to thank the numerous evangelical organizations (listed
elsewhere) that sent me up-to-date information concerning their ministries, and also a group of friends without whose help and encouragement
this book could not have been written—Joy and Davie Napier, Ginny and
Walter Hearn, Donald W. Dayton, Ted Brackman, Eric Evans, Ken
Sehested, Carol and Dave Andersen, Bob Rankin, Becky Manley, Tom
Garber, and my editor, Roy M. Carlisle, in particular. Oh, by the way, I
too am an evangelical.

RICHARD QUEBEDEAUX

Berkeley, California
July 1977

Part I

INTRODUCTION

1

The New Evangelical Majority

The evangelicals are a talking point everywhere. Their growing churches, highly visible campus and youth ministries, phenomenally successful publishing and other media efforts, and unlikely "twice-born" national celebrities, such as Charles Colson, Jeb and Gail Magruder, Johnny Cash, Anita Bryant, Graham Kerr (the Galloping Gourmet), Eldridge Cleaver, and Jimmy Carter have caught the eye of Protestant liberals, Roman Catholics, and secular journalists. Meanwhile, the new social and political activism of younger evangelicals has been a great encouragement to burned-out liberal and radical theologians and denominational–ecumenical leaders. Magazine writer Garry Wills insists that "evangelical chic" is impending.

In a widely publicized survey based upon in-person interviews with more than 1500 adults (18 and over) in more than 300 scientifically selected localities in the United States during August 27–30, 1976, The Gallup Poll discovered that one person in three (34 percent) has been *born again*—that is, has had a turning point in his or her life marked by a commitment to Jesus Christ. This figure works out to nearly 50 million American adults. Among Protestants alone, nearly half (48 percent) declare that they are born-again Christians. And 18 percent of Catholics also admit that they have had a born-again experience.

The poll found out that a very high proportion of twice-born Christians believe either that the Bible is the actual word of God and is to be taken literally, word for word, or at least that the Scriptures are the inspired word of God, although not everything in them should be taken literally. In the general population 38 percent of Americans polled (46 percent of the Protestants, 31 percent of the Catholics) affirm that the Bible is the actual word of God, to be taken literally; another 45 percent (42 percent of the Protestants, 55 percent of the Catholics) accept the Scriptures as the inspired word of God but do not believe that everything therein is to be taken literally.

According to The Gallup Poll, born-again Christians are eager to witness to their faith, a major reason that their churches are experiencing a striking growth in membership. Nationwide, 47 percent of all Americans polled (58 percent of the Protestants, 38 percent of the Catholics) have tried, at least once, to encourage someone to believe in Jesus Christ or to accept him as his or her Savior.

In the total sample 18 percent of those polled (1) have had a born-again experience; (2) hold a literal interpretation of the Bible (or accept its absolute authority); *and* (3) witness to their faith.[1]

On the basis of this survey-research data, George Gallup Jr., termed 1976 *the year of the evangelical.* Commenting on the aforementioned poll and other recent, more general surveys of religious life in America conducted by his organization, Gallup suggests that the United States may be in an early stage of a profound religious revival, with born-again Christians providing a powerful thrust.

The Gallup Poll recorded a rise in church attendance for 1976 for the first time in almost two decades, with 42 percent of Americans attending church or synagogue in a typical week. Church membership was also on the upswing in 1976, with seven in ten Americans describing themselves as church members. At the same time, six in ten said that their religious beliefs are "very important" in their lives. These gains have been accompanied by a great deal of interest on the part of the public in "experiential" religion. The Gallup Poll estimates that a projected six million Americans are involved in Transcendental Meditation (TM), five million in yoga, three million in mysticism, three million in charismatic renewal, and two million in Eastern religious traditions. And it is important to note here that participation by individuals in any one of these movements does not necessarily conflict with their involvement in organized religion.

Many of the participants are active members of traditional churches as well.

Gallup puts forward a number of factors that might explain the new religious consciousness in American life. First, he sees a turning *inward* among people seeking refuge from the pressures of everyday existence in a technological society. Second, he discerns a widespread search among Americans for nonmaterial values in the light of the disappointments of the material world and the fading of the "American dream." Third, Gallup credits President Carter's open discussion and practice of his own personal religious beliefs for the current focusing of attention on religion, particularly on the evangelical movement. Fourth, he points to the normal upswing following a decline in religious interest and activity (a typical American phenomenon). And fifth, he underscores the efforts of many clergy to make religion more appealing to young people and to satisfy their spiritual hunger; indeed, the growth of religious interest and activity, while across the board in terms of population groups, is centered largely among young adults.

On the basis of his empirical data, Gallup maintains that the United States is the most religious country in the world among the "advanced" nations surveyed; we have *both* a high level of formal education and a high level of religious belief and practice. Yet, citing our very bad record in terms of criminal victimization, consumer fraud, political corruption, tax cheating, bribery, and other evils, he feels that Americans as a whole may be only superficially religious. Religion may be increasing its influence, but, according to Gallup, morality is losing its hold. Hard evidence suggests a wide gap between religious belief and practice. Moreover, Gallup has found that the prayer life of many Americans is rudimentary and underdeveloped, and there is a "shocking" ignorance among Americans regarding even the basic doctrines and history of their own churches.

Yet Gallup is optimistic. Although many Americans, he believes, can be aptly described as spiritual illiterates and far from spiritual maturity, the fresh evidence of spiritual intensity and the desire for deeper religious commitment together indicate that Americans may now be entering a period of religious adolescence on the way to ultimate maturity. The marks of spiritual adulthood in a given person, Gallup maintains, might well include: (1) a constant awareness of the need to grow spiritually; (2) the desire to cultivate a deep inner life; (3) openness to new ways of finding God and tolerance of different ways; (4) a strong inclination to integrate a life of prayer with a life of service; and (5) the willingness to take a position *against* society if one's religious convictions so dictate.

Gallup feels that the shape of the future depends, to a large degree, on the religious belief and practice of two key groups in American society—the college educated, who include a high proportion of opinion leaders in the wider society, and the young, who will set the tone for church and nation in the years ahead. Although young people have a far poorer record of church attendance than their elders, for many of them God is still very much alive. Gallup believes that the young (even in "the spiritual 70s") do have a strongly developed social conscience, with many of them hoping to enter the helping professions, including social work. They still think (as in "the activist 60s") that the churches ought, as a high priority, to care for the sick, the poor, and the elderly, not just with their money but with their time, energy, and prayers. Gallup seems convinced that if religious leaders can motivate young people to blend their widespread will to believe with their desire to serve humanity, the current religious revival may indeed have lasting significance.[2] Among the evangelicals, at least, this has already begun to happen.

WHO ARE THE EVANGELICALS?

The evangelicals are the theme of this book. The word evangelical comes from the Greek *euangelion,* the evangel, or good news. Broadly speaking, an evangelical is a person who is devoted to the good news that God has sent us a Savior and that we can be partakers of God's redemptive grace in Jesus Christ. The Christian evangel is summarized in I Corinthians 15:1–4 (NEB):

> And now, my brothers, I must remind you of the gospel I preached to you; the gospel which you received, on which you have taken your stand, and which is now bringing you salvation. Do you still hold fast the Gospel as I preached it to you? If not, your conversion was in vain.
>
> First and foremost, I handed on to you the facts which had been imparted to me: that Christ died for our sins, in accordance with the scriptures; that he was buried; that he was raised to life on the third day, according to the scriptures. . . .

Historically, the term *evangelical* has taken on different meanings in divergent cultural contexts. It has applied since the Reformation to the

Protestant churches by reason of their claim to base their teaching preeminently on the Gospel, the "good news." The word sometimes signifies all the Protestant churches in Germany. It is also used in Germany and Switzerland to distinguish the Lutheran group of Protestant churches (Evangelical) as contrasted with the Calvinist (Reformed) group. In the United States, evangelical most often refers to the school of theology that lays special stress on personal conversion and salvation by faith in the atoning death of Christ.

In *The Young Evangelicals,* I defined an evangelical as a person who attests to the truth of, and acts upon, three major theological principles: (1) the full authority of Scriptures in matters of faith and practice; (2) the necessity of personal faith in Jesus Christ as Savior and Lord (conversion); and (3) the urgency of seeking the conversion of sinful men and women to Christ (evangelism). As we have already seen, about one in five Americans, the "hard-core evangelicals" (as designated by Gallup), share these three affirmations together, though many others are committed to one or two of the principles. It is with this understanding of the word that I shall consider the evangelicals.

Technically speaking, then, evangelical Christianity is a comprehensive term referring to that group of believers who accept the absolute authority of the Bible, have been converted to Christ (are born again), and who share their faith with others. Within this somewhat inclusive religious grouping, however, we can discern at least three highly visible subcultures, the members of which work out their salvation in radically different ways—the fundamentalists, the charismatics, and the direct descendants of the neo-evangelicals.

The fundamentalists constitute the strict subculture within evangelical Christianity. As a movement, fundamentalism emerged at the turn of the century and took on recognizable form after World War I. The name of the still-thriving movement is derived from a series of twelve short books entitled *The Fundamentals* (1910–15), written by a number of prominent theological conservatives and distributed widely throughout the English-speaking world. These doctrinal tracts were penned in defense of traditional orthodoxy, which was being challenged in the Protestant seminaries and denominational hierarchies by the gradual acceptance of biblical criticism, evolutionary theory, and the Social Gospel. By way of reaction, fundamentalism became an *opposition* movement against the modernists (or liberals) who had departed from orthodox belief; it was in that opposition that fundamentalists found their identity. They have insisted on the verbal inerrancy of Scripture and its literal interpretation. But the fundamentalists have also tended to live in a cultural time warp, rejecting almost all of the values not only of religious modernism· or liberalism but also of the wider society itself. For them there is not much difference between religious liberalism and out-and-out secularism.

The charismatics represent a second major subculture within evangelical Christianity. Participants in charismatic renewal (whose name is derived from the Greek *charismata,* gifts) are generally orthodox in belief, are born-again Christians, and witness to their faith. Their religious identity, however, is not centered so much on the defense of doctrinal formulations as it is on the experience and testimony that precede doctrine. The charismatic experience—most often seen as subsequent to conversion—is termed *baptism in the Holy Spirit* (after the pattern in the Book of Acts), by which a believer, in the course of prayer, is "filled with the Spirit" and receives one or more of the spiritual gifts mentioned by Paul in I Corinthians 12–14 and elsewhere in the New Testament. Charismatics usually feel that the ability to "speak in tongues" as a prayer language (one of the gifts cited and practiced by Paul) is the best evidence of Spirit baptism. Other prominent gifts emphasized within charismatic renewal include divine healing and prophecy. The movement itself is a more middle-class expression of the older "classical" pentecostalism, which is still thriving and from which charismatic renewal descends. Pentecostalism, very much akin to fundamentalism doctrinally and culturally, arose at the turn of the century and gets its name from the Day of Pentecost, when the church was founded and the Holy Spirit became manifest for the first time. The pentecostals, like the fundamentalists, formed their own very exclusive denominations. Charismatics, however, tend to remain in or join churches that are part of an historic denomination, hoping, by the practice of their spiritual gifts in the life of that church, to become a force for denominational renewal. (On pentecostalism and charismatic renewal, see my book, *The New Charismatics: The Origins, Development, and Significance of Neo-Pentecostalism.*)

A third major subculture within evangelical Christianity is represented by the direct descendants of fundamentalism, who first called themselves neo-evangelicals. These Christians broke with the stricter fundamentalists in the early 40s, reaffirming the basic tenets of orthodoxy, but rejecting what they saw in fundamentalism as theological and cultural excesses—anti-intellectualism, sectarianism, social unconcern, and an almost complete repudiation of the values of the wider society. In the 60s and 70s, the term *neo-evangelical* has generally been replaced by the more historic and inclusive designation, evangelical. These evangelicals created their own distinctive subculture and lifestyle; and to the American public at large, *they* are the evangelicals. Although I shall refer at times in this work to both the charismatics and the fundamentalists, attention will be directed primarily to the neo-evangelical subculture of the more comprehensive evangelical movement—its changing theology, leadership, and patterns of behavior. (For a brief historical survey of the development of fundamentalism and evangelicalism in the United States, see *The Young Evangelicals,* pp. 1–41).

2

New Trends,
New Tensions

Building upon the work of the eminent anthropologist Bronislaw Malinowski, H. Richard Niebuhr, in his classic study, *Christ and Culture*, defines culture as the artificial, secondary environment that men and women superimpose on the natural order. It is made up of language, habits, ideas, beliefs, customs, social organization, inherited artifacts, technical processes, and values. This social heritage is what the New Testament writers often had in mind when they spoke of *the world*.

Culture is always social. It is the organization of human beings into permanent groups. Culture and social existence are integrally related. Culture is also human achievement, distinguished from nature by evidence of human purpose and effort. It is the work of human minds and hands. Furthermore, since human achievements are all designed for an end or ends, the world of culture is always a world of values. What men and women make, we must assume, is intended for a purpose; it is designed to serve some ultimate good. The values with which these human achievements are concerned are predominantly those of what is good for people. In a word, what is good is what is good for people.

Culture is centered on the temporal and material realization of values. It would be wrong, however, to think of culture as inherently materialistic in the sense that what men and women work to achieve is always the satisfaction of their needs as physical and temporal beings. Human beings in culture do seek to gain nonmaterial or spiritual values; but even nonmaterial goods must be realized in temporal and material form. In addition, culture is almost as much concerned with the conservation of values as with their realization—for good reason. The customs and artifacts made by human minds and hands cannot be maintained unless people devote much of their effort to conservation. Culture is social tradition that can be preserved only by painful struggle against the revolutionary and critical powers in human life and reason that would destroy it. Finally, all culture is characterized by pluralism. The values a culture seeks to realize in any one time and place are many in number, because men and women are many. All individuals are complex personalities who have their own special claims and interests.[1]

In his very important book, *A Nation of Behavers,* religious historian Martin E. Marty argues that although many Americans think of their nation as a secular, pluralistic society, the vast majority still use religion as a means of establishing identity, connecting behavior with belief to overcome the unsettling and erosive effects of pluralism. If America is indeed a nation of believers (as The Gallup Poll tells us), then it has also become a nation of behavers. And for Marty what distinguishes one religious group from another is social behavior—what people do, the customs they observe, their culture—not only what they say or believe.

American pluralism is bewildering. Marty agrees with psychologist and historian Robert Jay Lifton, who speaks of an historical or psychohistorical "dislocation," a break in the sense of connection men and women have in the past felt with vital and nourishing symbols of their cultural traditions revolving around family, idea systems, religion, and the life cycle in general. People may regard these symbols as irrelevant, but they cannot avoid carrying them within or being affected by them. Likewise, the flooding of imagery produced by the extraordinary flow of nontraditional cultural influences over the mass media alters people's religious sensibilities as well. The images media convey cross over all boundaries until individuals can no longer maintain any clear boundaries at all. Thus they become prone to engage in an endless series of experiments and explorations, some shallow, some profound, each of which can be easily abandoned in favor of still new religious or psychological quests. Ultimately, the same individuals may experience the well-known and much talked about identity crisis.[2] (Small wonder, then, that so many Americans in search of identity are going back to their "roots"—a time, place, and culture where life held together and made sense.) That the evangelicals, no less than others, are now experiencing this trauma is suggested by the title of evangelical elder statesman Carl F. H. Henry's recent book, *Evangelicals in Search of Identity*.

The influence of the wider culture on the contemporary evangelical movement has been nothing less than staggering. Marty is correct in declaring that the evangelicals are making more and more compromises with the larger culture. Most people outside the evangelical community itself, however, are totally unaware of the profound changes that have occurred within evangelical Christianity during the last several years in the movement's understanding of the inspiration and authority of Scripture, its social concerns, its ecumenical posture, the nature of its emerging leadership, and its cultural attitudes generally. Only a decade ago it would have been nearly impossible to imagine the degree to which this metamorphosis has now actually taken place. Evangelicals today face the toughest of all religious problems: In what way or degree is Christ relevant to the situation in which the Christian must live? How can a follower of Jesus Christ be "in the world but not of it"? This is the question of Christ and culture.

Upward Social Mobility: Success and More Success

When fundamentalism emerged as a movement in the United States, it did so as a persecuted minority group. The fundamentalists rejected and were rejected by the increasingly liberal and inclusive denominations in which they had been nurtured. They formed their own exclusive denominations as well as missionary, relief, and evangelistic associations to proclaim and help them live out the truth of the Gospel as they understood it. The fundamentalists founded their own day schools, Bible institutes, colleges, seminaries, and youth organizations to preserve and defend the orthodox faith they cherished, to educate and nourish their children and future ministers free from the corruption of the world, its values and practices (including such worldly activities as drinking, smoking, dancing, attending the theater and movies, and playing cards, regularly denounced by the revivalists as the work of the devil). And they established their own radio programs, publishing houses, and magazines to help them disseminate the word to their own people and others they hoped to reach. Thus the fundamentalists believed in the Christ *against* culture.

The neo-evangelicals broke with fundamentalism in the early 40s, because the world was passing them by, and they were no longer convinced that the world is that bad after all—at least, not as bad as the fundamentalists had maintained. But they moved cautiously in the world through the 40s, 50s, and 60s. For three decades the evangelicals were hardly less persecuted than the fundamentalists. Indeed, Protestant liberals and the secular public did not even notice the difference between the fundamentalists and evangelicals. It took a long time for the evangelicals to really break away from the (largely working-class) cultural ghetto of fundamentalism and join the ranks of mainstream society. Quite frankly, the basic theology and behavior of fundamentalists and evangelicals remained very similar until the 70s.

Evangelicals decided to enter the world to change it—a world that could no longer take the message and lifestyle of fundamentalism seriously, if it ever did in the past. They began to affirm the Christ who *transforms* culture. The evangelicals knew that to influence the world for Christ they would have to gain its attention in a positive way. In a word, they would have to become *respectable* by the world's standards. And in this effort the evangelicals have been most successful.

In 1947 Fuller Theological Seminary was founded by evangelical leaders as a counterpart, with high intellectual standards, to the major liberal Protestant denominational and ecumenical graduate schools of theology. For many reasons it has been a controversial institution from the beginning. Few people remember that the first big controversy surrounding the seminary had to do with the "high" salaries its first professors were paid—about $7500 annually. In those days evangelicals looked askance at that kind of earnings for their leaders. Today, however, it is not particularly uncommon for pastors of large evangelical and charismatic congregations with multi-million-dollar facilities to earn as much as doctors and lawyers, dress in the height of fashion, live in very expensive homes (if not mansions), and drive the finest cars. A few of them even have their own airplanes.

Fuller's initial faculty held doctorates from some of the best universities and seminaries in America. As time went on, other evangelical colleges and schools of theology also began to recruit professors with equally impressive academic credentials. Existing campuses were enlarged and modernized. New institutions were established. (Oral Roberts University, a charismatic foundation that became fully accredited in only a few years' time, now has a campus valued in excess of $125 million and is building a medical school, dental school, nursing school, law school, business school, and school of theology.) Evangelicals started sending their sons and daughters to secular colleges and universities as well as to their own schools. Today evangelical fellowship groups at such universities as Harvard and Stanford are among the best attended and most significant student organizations on campus.

Billy Graham, who launched his ministry in a revival tent in Los Angeles in 1949, became an international celebrity in the 50s, and a friend and chaplain to presidents. Evangelicals began to "make it big" in business and the professions, forming their own professional and business fellowship organizations. Evangelical women attended Christian women's clubs and Christian charm schools. Television stars, professional athletes, musicians, beauty queens, and political figures became born-again Christians. Evangelical publishing houses, record companies, and television programs turned into multi-million-dollar industries. And now an avowed evangelical occupies The White House.

In the course of establishing their respectability in the eyes of the wider society, the evangelicals have become harder and harder to distinguish from other people. Upward social mobility has made the old revivalistic taboos dysfunctional. Evangelical business people, professionals, clergy, and students began traveling the world and soon discovered born-again believers in Europe, Africa, and Asia who drink and smoke—something American evangelicals had been told since childhood was wrong. They changed their minds. Furthermore, evangelical business people, professionals, and celebrities gradually found it necessary (and pleasant) to travel the cocktail-party circuit in Beverly Hills, San Marino, San Francisco, Dallas, Scarsdale, and Washington, D.C., and the cocktails became increasingly difficult to refuse. Evangelical young people learned how to dance and openly "grooved" on rock music. Professors in evangelical colleges and seminaries took up pipe smoking just like their liberal and secular colleagues. And evangelical magazines and newspapers began reviewing plays and movies.

Intellectual Sophistication: Growing Openness to Science, Biblical Criticism, and Broad Cultural Analysis

The key to understanding the new intellectual sophistication of the evangelicals is simple: more and better education. With the proliferation of faculty with the best doctorates in every academic discipline teaching at evangelical seminaries and colleges, it is small wonder that these same institutions have been profoundly influenced by the scholarship produced and taught at the most prestigious secular universities. Evolutionary theory, in a theistic context, is now taken for granted by many evangelical scientists. There are evangelical scholars in almost all academic disciplines, including the behavioral sciences—sociologists and psychologists who are active, and sometimes eminent, members of the leading professional societies in their respective fields. Fuller Seminary's School of Psychology is highly respected by secular psychiatrists and psychologists, and admission to its Ph.D. program is very competitive indeed. A few evangelical and charismatic churches even have a staff psychologist who provides services beyond the competence of their clergy.

Faculty members of Fuller's School of World Mission are engaged in highly sophisticated cross-cultural studies and are publishing important research in anthropology and sociology, some of it surprisingly radical. Biblical criticism has now made inroads in almost all evangelical colleges and seminaries. In fact, a few evangelical biblical scholars actually stand to the left of their liberal counterparts on some points.

Because most evangelical congregations and denominations as a whole are still much more conservative in their general orientation than their own educational institutions, it is becoming more and more difficult to recruit young pastors who have not been deeply influenced both by biblical criticism and by the behavioral sciences. This influence is reflected not only in the way these pastors preach but also in their teaching and counseling and in their understanding of evangelism. The Bible, once the *sole* intellectual tool for many evangelical ministers, has now been supplemented in their churches by serious theology, psychology, and sociology.

The Permissive Society

The permissive society, nurtured by the counterculture of the 60s, is probably here to stay. Sex is available premaritally, extramaritally, and nonmaritally to more and more Americans. One eminent researcher reports that for the present generation of young Americans, age 18 to 25, premarital intercourse runs as high as 81 percent for females and 95 percent for males. Extramarital sex is reported by almost half the males,

and one out of five women. Divorce has become easy, and it is now
"A-OK." According to a United States Census Bureau report, 37 percent
of first marriages and 59 percent of second marriages will end in divorce.[3]
And it seems that in some areas of the country there are more unmarried
couples, age 20 to 30, say, living together than married couples.
Homosexual lifestyles, at least in many major urban centers, are becoming more acceptable. Pornography, in an almost infinite variety of forms
geared to diverse tastes, is readily available not only in "adult"
bookstores and movie houses but also in sidewalk vending machines. Sex
for sale is found easily, and legal abortions can be obtained by anyone. As
we have already seen, nontraditional media images—television programs and advertising in general, for instance, stressing the acceptability
of sex outside marriage—are bombarding us with increasing regularity.
And popular magazines insist that if you aren't "getting off," something
is wrong with you.

The Gallup Poll is correct in asserting that born-again Christians "believe in a strict moral code."[4] But that strictness has been considerably
modified during the last few years, a direct result, I feel, of the continuing
advance of the permissive society. Sex in marriage alone is still the ideal
for most evangelicals—and it is celebrated. (It is interesting to note the
plethora of highly explicit books on sex technique in marriage written by
evangelicals and released by evangelical publishing houses. These books
rejoice in the demise of the once mandatory "missionary position," and
sanction, if not encourage, even *oral* sex.) Evangelical young people are,
without a doubt, far more conservative in their sex lives than their religious liberal and secular counterparts. But the monthly question and
answer column (patterned after "Dear Abby") in *Campus Life,* Youth for
Christ's magazine, gives the impression that more born-again high school
age couples are having intercourse than is generally supposed.

Among evangelical young people, masturbation is now often seen as a
gift from God. Divorce and remarriage are becoming more frequent and
acceptable among evangelicals of all ages, even in some of their more
conservative churches. This new tolerant attitude toward divorce has
been greatly facilitated both by the publication of positive articles and
books on the problem by evangelical authors and by the growth of ministry to singles in evangelical churches. Even very traditional pastors have
had to rethink their negative position on divorce in ministering to singles,
because in some singles groups in evangelical congregations there are

more divorced people than never-marrieds, and new partnerships regularly emerge out of those groups, with divorced individuals wanting to be remarried in their church. This poses a real problem for pastors who have traditionally refused to marry divorced people, especially when the former spouse is still alive.

Some evangelical women are taking advantage of abortion on demand. Many younger evangelicals occasionally use profanity in their speech and writing (though they are generally careful to avoid traditional profanity against the deity). Some of the recent evangelical sex-technique books assume that their readers peruse and view pornography on occasion, and they do. Finally, in 1976 there emerged a fellowship and information organization for practicing evangelical lesbians and gay men and their sympathizers. There is probably just as high a percentage of gays in the evangelical movement as in the wider society. Some of them are now coming out of the closet, distributing well-articulated literature, and demanding to be recognized and affirmed by the evangelical community at large. This breakthrough event is the result not only of gay liberation but also of the new acknowledgment in evangelical circles of the worth of singleness and of feminism. Gay evangelicals are reinterpreting the Old Testament and Pauline injunctions against homosexual practice. They have a high view of the authority of Scripture and insist that they are obedient to what it *really* demands.

Taking the Here and Now Seriously: From Conversion Alone to Public Discipleship

Traditionally, modern evangelical theology has been centered on the hereafter, the world to come. Conversion to Christ opened up the gates of heaven to believers, but it did little else. Although the neo-evangelicals, in breaking with the fundamentalists, did express, as early as the 40s, a new social conscience and a desire for evangelical involvement in the political, economic, and social life of the world, it was not until the 70s that they really got off the ground on this issue.

In the early 70s, if not a bit before then, a small group of evangelical young people (and a few of their elders) in a number of areas of the United States began to react strongly to the pie-in-the-sky by-and-by theological stance held by most evangelical churches, pastors, and lay people at the time. These *young evangelicals,* as I have termed them, had been deeply influenced by the rapid and profound cultural change that developed in the activist 60s and is still taking place. Some of them had been active in the civil rights struggle, the counterculture and the Jesus movement, the antiwar protests, even the New Left. They began viewing the Bible as their chief authority for radical social action and commitment to justice and peace. For them the Scriptures were no longer merely a guidebook on how to be "saved" and how to preserve the political status quo. Furthermore, the young evangelicals started repudiating what the martyred German theologian and pastor Dietrich Bonhoeffer had called *cheap grace,* and what others have termed *cheap conversion.* They linked conversion with discipleship—*public* discipleship—faith taken into the marketplace and used in the perpetual struggle against the principalities and powers, the evil structure of society. Thus some evangelicals at least have disavowed the recent history of their tradition by taking the here and now seriously, by recognizing what Christians have always known, "God so loved *the world.* . . ."

To be sure, the vanguard of what I have called a revolution in orthodoxy is still centered primarily on a small, highly literate, zealous elite, many of whose spokespersons hammered out the Chicago Declaration of Evangelical Social Concern in 1973. The influence of these younger evangelicals is no longer restricted to seminaries, colleges, and campus ministries alone. Increasingly, albeit slowly, it is being felt even within the institutional bastions of the evangelical establishment itself— the National Association of Evangelicals, the Billy Graham Evangelistic Association, the Evangelical Theological Society—and in the congregations and ministries of distinctively evangelical denominations, from the Southern Baptist Convention to The Lutheran Church–Missouri Synod, from the Christian Reformed Church to the Assemblies of God.

Seeing God in the Secular

In 1965 Harvey Cox stunned the religious world with the publication of his highly controversial book, *The Secular City.* The American Baptist theologian argued that *secularization,* properly understood, should not be considered the enemy of the people of God; rather, it ought to be viewed as the logical outcome of biblical faith. For Cox secularization represented the historical process by which society and culture are freed from tutelage to religious control and closed metaphysical world views. He felt strongly that the religious culture that had dominated our society was characterized preeminently by superstition and the "tyranny" of legalistic religious authority. This culture was ceremonial, other-worldly, and provincial, and existed in sharp contrast to the secular city that represents a new and fulfilling style of life—urban, technological, pluralistic, and secular. Cox maintained that the world, not the church, is the proper locus of Christian life. God has revealed himself in his mighty acts in history, not in ritualism and metaphysical concepts. In fact, the world of politics is a primary sphere of God's liberating work today. God wants the service of Christians not merely in some small sector of life termed religious but in the whole sweep of secular activity. (Secularization, however, must not be confused with *secularism,* an attitude of total indifference to religious institutions and practices and even to religious questions, in which science becomes the only trustworthy path to knowledge.)

Cox, whose ideas were radical at the time, should not be identified with the "Death of God" theologians. In *The Secular City,* God was seen to be very much behind and involved in the secularization process. Like Bonhoeffer, Cox affirmed a "religionless Christianity" that calls for an end to the traditional distinction between the sacred and the secular realms, with religion being confined to the sacred realm alone. In other words, the world is the concrete historical context where that which is transcendent and ultimate can be experienced in the midst of the worldly and penultimate.[5]

In Cox's opinion secularization demands that men and women turn their attention away from other worlds toward this one. We have already seen that many evangelicals are shifting their focus from the hereafter to the here and now, stressing time rather than eternity. Their firm rejection of legalistic religious authority and metaphysical abstractions is readily apparent. Indeed, we can discern very little, if any, reference to heaven and hell (except existentially) in young evangelical publications. Building a just society and developing ethical living here and now seem far more important than preparing people for heaven.

But the secular theologians of the 60s, including Cox, were wrong at some points. Urban life has proved to be less fulfilling than they envisioned. Technological advance has been a disappointment as well—instead of liberating men and women it has tended to dehumanize them by depriving them of an identity and reducing them to an economic entity at best and exploited and tortured victims at worst. Furthermore, as The Gallup Poll has shown, modern Americans still demonstrate that they have very profound religious needs and aspirations. "Secular man" turned out to be far less secular than theologians had supposed. Nevertheless, at the same time that many repentant Protestant liberals and radicals of the 60s are turning inward again in the 70s—back to metaphysical speculation and deep spirituality—evangelicals may be going in the other direction. In fact, some of them appear just about ready to celebrate the secular city, more than a decade too late.

The Universalist Impulse

I have suggested that the nontraditional images of modern culture carried by the contemporary mass media cross over all boundaries, with the result that individuals find it increasingly difficult to maintain any clear ideological and social perimeters at all. Despite the mental and emotional turmoil caused by the collapse of these limits, however, there remains in modern Western society a great reluctance to create new boundaries, to keep people out.

In Protestant liberalism and neo-orthodoxy, it has generally been held that *all* men and women are saved and have already been reconciled to God, whether they know and acknowledge that fact or not. God, being perfect in mercy and love, could not possibly condemn any of his creatures to endless torment and separation from his presence in hell. Thus liberals and the neo-orthodox turned away from traditional world mission and evangelism. If personal conversion to Christ isn't necessary, in an absolute sense, why bother with missionaries and evangelists commissioned to win converts? Dialogue with men and women of "living faiths" replaced the once urgent attempt of Christians to convert members of other religious traditions.

Evangelicals, however, resisted the tendency of Protestant liberalism and neo-orthodoxy to affirm universal salvation. First, they insisted that this doctrine is incompatible with biblical teaching on the matter of salvation. Jesus is the *only* way to God, and God requires *all* people to repent and accept his provision for salvation in Christ. God is indeed a God of love and mercy, but he is a God of justice as well. Second, evangelicals felt that universalism inevitably saps the life and vitality of the church by dispensing with traditional mission work and evangelism. Without the urgent call to conversion, the church would decline in memberhip and eventually die.

I do not want to infer that contemporary evangelicals are consciously becoming universalists. But certain discernible trends suggest that there has been a subtle shift in that direction among some leading evangelical intellectuals and activists at least. In ''Why Is Jesus the Only Way?,'' a very controversial article in the December 1976 issue of *Eternity,* Clark Pinnock, a highly respected younger evangelical theologian, argued that, either at death or in some other way, God will save those who have truly sought him and who have not heard the Gospel. The evangelical missionary thrust has been motivated largely by the belief that, apart from accepting the Gospel, which people must *hear* to accept, the heathen are lost. Pinnock, obviously, would like to give a second chance to the sincere seekers after God who have never heard of Jesus Christ.

Young evangelical activists, who rarely speak of heaven and hell, are reinterpreting the task of evangelism so that it looks to the casual observer more like the call to social justice and peace than the traditional call to conversion, personal regeneration through Christ. This is not to say that these younger evangelicals have abandoned their belief in the necessity of personal conversion; they still affirm that demand. But, as we saw earlier, the emphasis of their work is building a just society on earth and developing ethical living here and now, rather than preparing men and women for heaven.

Finally, the new willingness of many evangelical academics, pastors, and activists to have fellowship and engage in cooperative activities with Protestant liberals (who may deny some of the cardinal tenets of orthodoxy) and Jews, without trying to convert them, makes it difficult to believe that these same evangelicals regard their not born-again colleagues as hell-bound sinners. Clearly, in the minds of such evangelicals, the boundaries between saved and lost have been obscured.

THE COLLAPSE OF THE ESTABLISHMENT EVANGELICAL SUBCULTURE AND THE BROADENING OF EVANGELICAL THEOLOGY

Just as Protestant liberals, Roman Catholics, and the secular public have discovered the evangelical subculture, that same subculture has begun to collapse. We have seen that evangelicals as a whole do constitute a sizable and distinctive subculture of the wider American society which itself can be broken down into numerous *smaller* subcultures, all of which affirm the full authority of Scripture, the need for conversion to Christ, and the mandate for evangelism, but differ markedly in their interpretation of these convictions and in lifestyle and behavior as well. (A subculture may be defined simply as the sum total of cultural regularities in any society or class of human beings smaller than the group of local communities that serves to define a culture.[6]) We have also noted that one of these subcultures, the direct descendants of the neo-evangelicals who first broke with fundamentalism, emerged in the 40s, 50s, and 60s as the dominant distinctive religious grouping within American evangelical Christianity in terms of visibility and influence. They appropriated the name evangelical for themselves alone and were recognized as *the evangelicals* by both the liberal religious media and the secular public. It is this particular subculture, which I have termed the evangelical establishment,[7] that is collapsing.

The chief symbols of the evangelical establishment have been the National Association of Evangelicals, the Evangelical Theological Society, Billy Graham, and *Christianity Today*. The NAE, a loose association of distinctively evangelical denominations, congregations, and individuals, was formed in 1942. The ETS, established in 1949, is a professional society and fellowship of evangelical scholars. Billy Graham, who needs no introduction here, launched his career as an evangelist of international stature in 1949. And *Christianity Today,* founded in 1956 with the help of Graham himself, has been the most important magazine of evangelical conviction; until recently it regularly mapped out the acceptable boundaries of evangelical theology and lifestyle in its editorials and in the majority of the articles it published. In addition to Graham, the following men have been among the most influential leaders of the evangelical establishment: Carl F. H. Henry, founding editor of *Christianity Today,* now lecturer-at-large for World Vision International; Harold Ockenga, former pastor of Park Street Church in Boston, now president of Gordon-Conwell Theological Seminary; Harold Lindsell, retired editor of *Christianity Today;* and Francis Schaeffer, author and culture critic.

Evangelicals—as represented by the evangelical establishment, that is—used to be easy to identify. Largely Baptists and Presbyterians, they were rational Calvinist scholastics, committed to the total inerrancy of Scripture and the propositional revelation contained therein. The Bible is completely free from error because it is God's inspired word, and God cannot lie or contradict himself. Biblical revelation is propositional in that God has expressed himself objectively and clearly in words, in language that must be believed as true, usually in its literal sense. This position is most at home in post-Reformation scholastic orthodoxy as mediated to modern evangelicalism by the nineteenth-century Old

Princeton theology typified by Charles Hodge, Archibald Alexander Hodge, and Benjamin B. Warfield. Many of these evangelicals were also avid premillennialists.

The evangelical establishment, led by white, middle-class males, identified itself totally with the cultural ethos of modern revivalism and its characteristic lifestyle and taboos epitomized in Billy Graham. The descendants of fundamentalism, these evangelicals were conservative Republicans as well. Liberal theology and liberal politics went together; in opposing one, it seemed logical to repudiate the other, too.

As a relatively homogeneous unit, the evangelical establishment never fully accepted and affirmed many born-again Christians who once again readily identify themselves as evangelicals. For instance, this subculture looked askance at the Arminians (e.g., Wesleyans and other "holiness" people), with their emphasis on free will, perfectionism, and what Calvinists viewed as "works righteousness." Arminians also play down doctrine too much for strict Calvinists. The evangelical establishment looked down upon strongly confessional Lutherans and Roman Catholics as well. They are too "ethnic," too sacramental, tradition-minded, and often high church. At the same time, the Christian Reformed Church (no less than Episcopalians, Lutherans, and Catholics) were virtually excluded. Their members drink beer and whiskey and smoke tobacco and who knows what else? The evangelical establishment found it equally difficult to accept pentecostals and charismatics, with their nonrational, subjective, and experience-oriented theology. The Spirit in charismatic renewal and pentecostalism is simply too unpredictable! And too bad for the Anabaptists (e.g., Mennonites and most Brethren) as well. They are pacifists and not middle-class enough in their lifestyles. Blacks and women, of course, were generally excluded (from leadership, at least). If the wider society did not take them seriously, why should the evangelical establishment? This is not to say that members of all these groups have not, at times, shared in the fellowship of the evangelical establishment (the NAE and ETS, for instance). They have indeed, but only to the degree that they have been willing to play down, if not deny, their distinctiveness—to pretend to be Calvinists, doctrinal scholastics, conservative Republicans, nonpacifists, and middle-class, white males, completely at home in the ethos of revivalism.

The question remains: Why is this religious subculture, the evangelical establishment, collapsing? The credit or blame can be given largely to the young evangelicals, highly visible Christians who, since 1970, began to identify with the groups that had been excluded by the evangelical establishment. The result has been that many Wesleyan, Lutheran, Roman Catholic, Christian Reformed, Episcopal, pentecostal, charismatic, black, and feminist Christian leaders now boldly identify with the young evangelicals who affirm *them*—to the point that they, too, proudly call themselves evangelicals. These people believe the Bible, are born again, and share their faith with others. Thus with the collapse of the old evangelical establishment subculture as the bastion of evangelical conviction, influence, and identity, we can discern the broadening of evangelical theology and the recognition of a wider evangelical culture, the likes of which is giving establishment evangelical elder statesmen like Schaeffer and Lindsell "culture shock" as they are confronted by a host of new evangelicals, many of whom differ from them dramatically in biblical interpretation, politics, lifestyle, and racial and ethnic background.

Part II

THE EVANGELICAL
RIGHT AND CENTER

At this point we shall take a comprehensive look at the spectrum of contemporary evangelical Christianity in the United States—leading personalities, distinctive denominations and churches, important organizations for fellowship, evangelism, and mission, and influential schools of thought within the movement—in order to understand the evangelicals more thoroughly and discern more adequately the effect of the wider culture on the movement, producing the new trends and tensions already observed. In so doing, I shall not treat the evangelical far right, the fundamentalists (who usually do not identify as evangelicals, anyway). And I shall give attention to the charismatics only when they represent poignant examples of the impact of the wider culture on the broad evangelical movement.

In discussing a spectrum of belief and behavior in any religious movement, we are forced—inevitably—to *label* both individuals and organizations that make up that movement. In the case of modern evangelical Christianity, such labeling has become a rather precarious enterprise. In the present "identity confusion" among evangelicals, many are in transition, moving from one stance to another (generally from right to center or left): some will resist the labels we choose; still others will repudiate labels altogether. Thus the attempt to categorize organizations and people must be taken with the knowledge that the designations selected are tentative, open to change, and that there will be more than a few exceptions to the generalizations we put forward.

In describing evangelical behavior and belief within the categories of right, center, and left, we have first to define what those rubrics mean in the context of evangelical Christianity as a whole. Clearly, the boundaries of these designations are very hard to delineate with accuracy. Nevertheless, we can say that the typical progression from right to left on the spectrum represents a change in position in terms of cultural and social behavior in general, politics and economics, *and* theology (though the authority of the Bible, the need for conversion, and the mandate for evangelism are affirmed—but interpreted differently—at both ends of the spectrum).

In economics and politics evangelicals of the right and center are most often conservative Republicans or, less often perhaps, conservative Democrats. They are committed capitalists and strict constructionists in their interpretation of the Constitution. Reformists among them are "gradualists," who oppose any radical upset of the status quo. In their social and cultural attitudes more generally, center and right evangelicals affirm the Protestant ethic, demand hard work of all who are able (including themselves), exalt the nuclear family and traditional male and female roles in church and society, look askance at the permissive society, and are very moderate (or abstainers) when it comes to worldly behavior that evangelicals once almost uniformly denounced—drinking, dancing, attendance at the theater and cinema, and the like.

3

Theological Convictions

Theologically, evangelicals of the right and center most often (but not always) believe in the total inerrancy of Scripture, not only in matters pertaining to salvation (faith and practice) but also in those relevant to history and the cosmos. They believe in a literal Adam and Eve, an historical "fall," and a creationist rather than an evolutionary explanation of the origins of humankind. The story of Jonah and the great fish is taken as historical fact, as are all the other accounts of extraordinary events in the Bible. For center and right evangelicals, any passage of Scripture is to be taken as true in its natural, literal sense unless the context of a passage itself indicates otherwise, or unless an article of faith established elsewhere in the Bible requires a broader understanding of the text. Extrabiblical linguistic and cultural considerations must never decide the interpretation of a given text. Indeed, right and center evangelicals tend to use Scripture to answer all questions (ideally, at least) and are very, very cautious when it comes to supplementing the absolute authority of the Bible with reason, experience, and the findings of the natural and behavioral sciences. Thus Schaeffer declares: "There is the danger of evangelicalism becoming less than evangelical, of its not really holding to the Bible as being without error in all that it affirms. . . . Holding to a strong view of Scripture [i.e., total inerrancy] or not holding to it is the watershed of the evangelical world."[1]

The intensity with which these beliefs are held and the strictness with which this behavior is acted out determine whether the designation *center* or *right* should be applied to individual evangelicals or their groups. Quite frankly, there is not a great deal of difference here between right and center. And it is these groupings that constitute the vast majority of the evangelical population in the United States at the present time.

The evangelical left—the young evangelicals and their sympathizers—will be treated in more detail later. In politics and economics they vary from moderate Republicans (welfare capitalists) to democratic socialists, if not Marxists. In their cultural and social attitudes more generally, left evangelicals affirm the nuclear family but also have a high regard for singleness and are open to alternative domestic lifestyles such as extended families and communes. Just about all of them are feminists to one degree or another, and some are activists in the struggle for equal rights for women in church and society. Drinking, smoking, dancing, movies, and the like pose few problems for the evangelical left (nor does the permissive society as a whole). Left evangelicals accept constructive, devout biblical criticism and the highly probable theories resulting from scientific research, which, in addition to reason and experience, are used to interpret the Bible—the fully authoritative guide for Christian faith and practice. Indeed, they tend to prefer the term *authoritative* as it is applied to Scripture to *inerrant* (the favorite of the right) or *infallible* (the more historic and centrist designation).

CENTERS OF THEOLOGICAL EDUCATION AND SCHOLARSHIP

Prior to the 60s, virtually all the seminaries and colleges associated with the neo-evangelicals and their descendants adhered to the total inerrancy understanding of biblical authority (at least they did not vocally express opposition to it). This position was reflected in the statements of faith held by many of these schools and subscribed to annually, without reservation, by all board members and faculty. But it is a well-known fact that a large number, if not most, of the colleges and seminaries in question now have faculty who no longer believe in total inerrancy, even in situations where their employers still require them to sign the traditional declaration that the Bible is "verbally inspired," "inerrant," or "infallible in the whole and in the part," or to affirm in other clearly defined words the doctrine of inerrancy that was formulated by the Old Princeton school of theology and passed on to fundamentalism. Some of these faculty interpret the crucial creedal clauses in a manner the original framers would never have allowed; others simply sign the affirmation with tongue in cheek. Of the seminaries and colleges that remain faithful to the total inerrancy position, two graduate schools of theology are especially prominent and can be considered leading centers of theological education and scholarship primarily for the evangelical right and center.

The first is Dallas Theological Seminary, located in Dallas, Texas. This nondenominational school of theology was founded in 1924, at the height of the fundamentalist-modernist controversy, by the noted conservative Presbyterian Bible teacher, Lewis Sperry Chafer, the seminary's first president. Dallas's current president, John F. Walvoord, feels equally at home with the tag *fundamentalist* or *evangelical*. He heads a graduate school of theology that was made up, in 1976–1977, of 52 full-time faculty and 775 resident students, representing 307 colleges and universities, 15 seminaries, 47 states, 14 foreign countries, and 70 denominational groups here and abroad.

Dallas Seminary pioneered in offering a standard four-year course for graduation, leading to the degree of Master of Theology, Th.M.. (The normal first professional degree in theology is the Master of Divinity, M.Div., completed after a three-year course.) Only *men* are admitted to the Th.M. program, which requires three years of Greek and two years of Hebrew and emphasizes systematic theology, Old Testament exegesis, New Testament exegesis, and Bible exposition. This course may well be the most traditional, highly structured, and academically demanding professional theological curriculum in the United States today.

Dallas occupies an impressive twelve-acre campus. Its students and faculty follow a strict dress code (jacket and tie are usually required), only recently modified, and standards of conduct that disallow "the use of tobacco and intoxicating liquor, and other questionable practices . . . not suitable for Christian leaders."[2]

Dallas Seminary has produced for the evangelical world not a few eminent pastors, teachers, missionaries, evangelists, administrators, writers, counselors, chaplains, and other religious professionals, some of whom have moved considerably to the left of the school's doctrinal and lifestyle stance. Its statement of faith is distinctively complete and detailed, making it extremely difficult to interpret away any of the statement's clauses. Affirming "the great fundamentals of the Christian faith" in the context of Calvinism and strict premillennial theology (dispensationalism), Dallas's statement of faith professes belief in the verbal, plenary inspiration of the Bible, the virgin birth and deity of Jesus Christ, His bodily resurrection, the sinful depraved nature of man, salvation by faith alone in the efficacious, substitutionary death of Christ, the imminency of the pretribulational rapture of the church, and the premillennial return of Christ.[3]

Dispensational theology, in fact, is and always has been the hallmark of Dallas Theological Seminary. Dispensationalism, as a coherent system of theology, originated in Great Britain during the early nineteenth century with the writings and ministry of J. N. Darby, founder of the Plymouth Brethren, and was popularized largely by the Scofield Reference Bible, first published in 1909. This school of theology divides history into several (often seven) ''dispensations'' of time, each of which signifies a different way in which God relates to humanity, and in which humanity utterly fails to please God. In dispensationalism a literal thousand-year millennial reign of Christ on earth is preceded by a seven-year tribulation, or time of woes, in which the Antichrist is revealed, and before which the church (all born-again Christians) is ''raptured,'' taken directly into the presence of God, until the beginning of the millennium.

A second leading center of theological education and scholarship for the evangelical center and right is Trinity Evangelical Divinity School, located in Deerfield, Illinois, a suburb of Chicago. Trinity, a seminary related to the Evangelical Free Church of America, but largely non-denominational in its stance, traces its origins back to 1884, when the Norwegian–Danish Department of Chicago Theological Seminary was opened (the Evangelical Free Church is rooted in Swedish-American pietism). The campus was moved to its present thiry-acre site in Deerfield in 1961. The school was restructured in 1963, and gained notoriety within evangelicalism when a few prominent professors left Fuller Seminary and joined the Trinity faculty to protest Fuller's departure from the total inerrancy position on Scripture.

In 1975 Trinity Evangelical Divinity School had a faculty of about 50 regular and visiting professors, teaching more than 400 full-time students from 41 states and 17 foreign countries, representing 64 denominational groups here and abroad and a wide variety of colleges, universities, and seminaries. More than 60 percent of Trinity's graduates regularly enter the pastoral ministry.

Throughout the 60s and 70s, Trinity has been regarded by many evangelicals as the best, more conservative, nondispensational (but premillennial) alternative to Fuller. Its brief statement of faith includes a summary of the most important doctrines of modern Calvinist orthodoxy; and, of course, biblical inerrancy is affirmed. "The Scriptures, both Old and New Testaments . . . [are] the inspired Word of God, without error in the original writings. . . ."[4] Unlike Dallas, however, Trinity admits women as well as men to its first professional degree program in theology (the standard M.Div. course is followed) and allows a significant measure of diversity among faculty and students in theology and lifestyle. Abstinence from the use of alcohol and tobacco, for instance, is not required, and there is no dress code.

EVANGELICAL THEOLOGICAL SOCIETY AND CARL F. H. HENRY

Since 1949 the Evangelical Theological Society has provided the major forum for the critical discussion of scholarship by the evangelical right and center. The inspiration for this association came initially from the faculty of Gordon Divinity School (now Gordon-Conwell Theological Seminary), who proposed that conservative scholars meet regularly for biblical and theological debate. In December 1949 a group of sixty evangelical academicians met in in Cincinnati to draft a constitution that brought the ETS into being. These men represented a wide variety of schools and affiliations. While denominational loyalties and doctrinal orientations were quite divergent (within the evangelical context at the time), there was no disposition to compromise on the one matter all the delegates considered of extreme importance—the inerrancy of the scriptures. Thus the creedal statement, signed then and now by every member of the society and made the sole condition for membership, was narrowed to this single fundamental: "The Bible alone and the Bible in its entirely is the word of God written, and therefore inerrant in the autographs." For the ETS biblical inspiration demanded inerrancy.

A major national meeting of the ETS is held annually. Like other gatherings of professional societies, it too is characterized by the reading of prepared paapers, by addresses, and by panel discussions to stimulate further research and debate. But this meeting of Christian scholars also includes informal discussion groups, "fellowship" at meals, and devotional periods. Smaller regional gatherings are convened at least annually (the United States and Canada are currently divided into seven regions, each chaired by a different person). Eminent evangelical elder statesmen who have served as president of the society include John F. Walvoord, Vernon Grounds (president of Conservative Baptist Theological Seminary), Kenneth Kantzer (former dean of Trinity Evangelical Divinity School, now editor of *Christianity Today*), Carl F. H. Henry, and Harold Lindsell.

Full membership is restricted to persons who hold at least the Th.M. or its equivalent (generally, the second professional degree in theology). Some of the papers read at the annual meeting are published in the quarterly *Journal of the Evangelical Theological Society*. In addition, a number of monographs written by members and others have been published to supplement the *Journal*.

Unfortunately, most of the scholarship produced by ETS members has not been impressive. In the words of Henry himself, "Those who declare the unabashed commitment to biblical inerrancy guarantees theological vitality have the past twenty-five years of meager production by the Evangelical Theological Society to explain."[5] Further more, it is widely known that the ETS is now in the midst of a struggle over its inerrancy statement, which some (probably many) members sign but no longer share.[6] The influence on even the venerable Evangelical Theological Society of the evangelical left—not to mention biblical criticism more generally—has been substantial and is increasing. Thus the society's future is clearly in doubt.

The one really distinguished religious thinker who, in good conscience, remains a member of ETS is Carl F. H. Henry himself. The author of more than twenty books and numerous symposia, he was recently described by *Time* as evangelicalism's "leading theologian" (February 14, 1977 p. 82). Henry's magnum opus, *God, Revelation and Authority* (the first two parts of a projected four-volume study had appeared by the end of 1976) attacks the subjectivism of—by Henry's standards—nonevangelical theologies and defends the use of reason as well as faith in theologizing. Not a work on systematic theology per se, it is restricted to the concept of revelation itself and the problems that gather around that concept. Indeed, Henry's study is the broadest, the most learned, and the most incisive and comprehensive work on revelation in the current evangelical tradition.

Henry, an American Baptist minister whose stance is thoroughly Reformed, insists in *God, Revelation and Authority* that God has given us an inerrant, propositional revelation in the Bible that stands up better than any other theological or philosophical position when evaluated by reason. For him all theological stances that are nonevangelical can be shown to be contradictory, and therefore false. Henry repudiates any position that accepts something by faith uncritically (such as some expressions of fundamentalism); any stance that appeals to religious experience apart from a serious interaction with reason (such as charismatic renewal); any stance that rests on an interior existential decision or encounter (such as neo-orthodoxy); and any kind of mysticism or nonpropositional view of revelation, since both bypass reason.[7]

In evaluating all the theological scholarship produced since the early 40s by thinkers of the evangelical center and right—so much of it grounded in the inerrancy doctrine—I have to agree that Henry's criticism is valid. The total production itself has been meager, offering little, if any, evidence of vitality of thought. Moreover, it is no longer just the liberal religious scholars who label the bulk of that work mediocre or anti-intellectual. These academicians are now joined by a host of evangelicals on the left who, with increasing regularity, put forward the same negative critiques in articles and reviews. This significant development, of course, provides evidence that the boundaries of what passes for evangelical theology are indeed broadening.

4

Church Organization

In a sense the modernists won the fundamentalist–modernist struggle. They gradually became dominant both in the seminaries and in the hierarchies of the so-called mainline Protestant denominations, such as The United Presbyterian Church in the U.S.A., The United Methodist Church, The Episcopal Church, the American Baptist Churches in the U.S.A., and the United Church of Christ. Although many theological conservatives remained members of these increasingly inclusive denominations, others forsook them to form their own more exclusive denominations or totally independent churches. But there are also two large denominations and a number of smaller ones (some of them ethnic in character), founded prior to the fundamentalist–modernist dispute, which remained relatively untainted by liberalism and continued to hold to a generally orthodox stance in theology.

Southern Baptist Convention

The largest distinctively evangelical denomination in the United States—and the largest of all Protestant denominations—is the Southern Baptist Convention (SBC), of which numerous prominent evangelicals (including Billy Graham, Harold Lindsell, and Jimmy Carter) are members. With more than 35,000 congregations—largely in the South, but more and more in northern, eastern, and western states as well—54,000 ordained clergy, and an inclusive membership over 12,500,000,[1] the SBC in now one of the fastest growing American denominations.

It was inevitable that Northern and Southern Baptists would split over the slavery issue, even before the outbreak of the Civil War. In May 1845 the Southern Baptist Convention was organized, establishing its own foreign and home mission boards. From the beginning the SBC has had a strong, clearly defined central structure (located in Nashville at the present time), though the Baptist principle of local autonomy has always remained intact. The convention meets annually, with an ever increasing number of delegates ("messengers") in attendance.

Twenty denominational agencies work with 33 state conventions in home and foreign mission enterprises, Sunday schools, educational institutions, and ministerial retirement services. The Home Mission Board, with 64 members, works across the United States and in Panama and the Panama Canal Zone, with more than 2200 missionaries in active service. It serves migrants in the South and Native Americans in the West and Southwest, working among several language groups and the deaf. The board also cooperates with black Baptist denominations, and provides loans for the erection of new church buildings.

Foreign missionaries of the Southern Baptist Convention are at work in 75 countries on 4 continents. The SBC has over 2500 active missionaries abroad, 660 schools supported by foreign mission programs, 6000 churches (and 6400 smaller chapels), 20 hospitals, and 150 clinics and dispensaries.

The Sunday School Board publishes literature for and supervises the work of over 7 million students (children through senior citizens) in over 33,500 Sunday schools. There are 7 theological seminaries in the SBC, with over 5500 students, 44 senior colleges and universities, 12 junior colleges, 8 academies, and 4 Bible schools. Circulation of Southern Baptist publications reached a figure of more than 109 million in 1972.

In matters of faith every Baptist congregation speaks for itself; but certain distinctively Baptist "doctrines" are held in common. The authority and inspiration of the Bible stands as the cornerstone of Baptist belief. The foundation of Baptist theology—ideally—is the commitment to follow New Testament faith and practice, with the dictates of one's own conscience as the interpreter. Believer's baptism by immersion and the Lord's Supper (interpreted symbolically) are practiced as "ordinances"; they do not have any role in a person's salvation.

Southern Baptists are generally, but not always, more conservative than their Northern (American) Baptist sisters and brothers in both theology and lifestyle—and more Calvinistic as well.[2] The use of tobacco and alcohol is frowned upon, though smoking is allowed in many sections of the tobacco-growing South. Despite the fact that the vast majority of increasingly middle-class Southern Baptists are good representatives of the evangelical right and center, the influence of the evangelical left (and, to a degree, theological liberalism) is certainly being felt, particularly in the convention's colleges, universities, and seminaries (Southeastern Baptist Theological Seminary, in Wake Forest, North Carolina; and Southern Baptist Theological Seminary in Louisville, Kentucky, most notably). Carl F. H. Henry maintains that the SBC "in several of its seminaries espouses a murky neoorthodoxy; [and] some of its colleges, no longer unapologetically Christian, even hire faculty members who make no profession of faith whatever."[3] Notable Southern Baptist churches at the left of the convention's theological spectrum include First Baptist Church, Chapel Hill, North Carolina; Myers Park Baptist Church, Charlotte; Second Ponce de Leon Baptist Church in Atlanta; and Broadway Baptist Church in Ft. Worth, Texas.

Social action concerns, characteristic of the evangelical left, are expressed and carried out with increasing vigor by the SBC's Christian Life Commission, headed by Foy Valentine, and the Texas Baptist Convention's Christian Life Commission, directed by James Dunn. First Baptist Church of San Antonio, Texas, pastored by SBC president Jimmy Allen, is probably the most prominent congregation in the SBC to have developed *both* an impressive and passionate social action program and an equally successful ministry of evangelism. For a distinctively evangelical denomination, the Southern Baptist Convention has displayed a good deal of openness to new ideas and novel forms of ministry, and it is becoming significantly more inclusive in its membership.

The Lutheran Church–Missouri Synod

The second major distinctively evangelical denomination that, until recently, weathered the fundamentalist–modernist controversy and its aftermath relatively unscathed is The Lutheran Church–Missouri Synod (LCMS). With over 5800 churches, 7300 ordained clergy, and an inclusive membership of over 2,750,000,[4] this constitutes the second largest Lutheran body in the United States. Originally (and still largely) an ethnic German denomination, the LCMS gets the *Missouri* in its name from the founding of the church in that state by Saxon immigrants, joined later by

Hanoverians in Indiana and Franconians in Michigan. From the beginning all three groups were firmly committed to the preservation of orthodox Lutheranism. They had fought the trend toward rationalism in Germany and had come to the United States for religious freedom, intending to form a synod (national structure) in which the sovereignty of the local congregation would be acknowledged. Organized in 1847, the Missouri Synod has its headquarters in St. Louis; it holds its general convention biennially.

The LCMS has always been keenly interested in education. The denomination operates 1177 parochial schools, 27 high schools, and 5889 day schools. It has 10 junior colleges, 3 teachers' colleges, and 1 university (Valparaiso University in Valparaiso, Indiana). The synod also operates two graduate schools of theology—Concordia Seminary in St. Louis and Concordia Seminary in Ft. Wayne, Indiana. Colleges and universities are served by the Department of Campus Ministry, with 100 full-time campus pastors and 70 others working on a part-time basis.

Overseas mission work is carried out in cooperation with sister churches in India, Sri Lanka, New Guinea, the Philippines, Taiwan, South Korea, Ghana, Nigeria, Hong Kong, and Lebanon. The LCMS has the most extensive ministry among the deaf in American Protestantism, with 44 full-time pastors serving 55 congregations.

Theologically, The Lutheran Church–Missouri Synod is indeed evangelical in character (right and center). However, it might be more appropriate to term the denomination *orthodox* and *strongly confessional*. The doctrinal standard of the LCMS—strictly enforced—is found in Scripture "as it was interpreted by the Book of Concord" plus the three ecumenical creeds (Apostles', Nicene, and Athanasian) and the six Lutheran confessions (the Augsburg Confession, the apology of the Augsburg Confession, the Smalcald Articles, the Formula of Concord, and the two catechisms of Martin Luther).[5] Unlike the SBC, the LCMS was hardly affected at all by the cultural ethos of revivalism. Its worship is highly liturgical and sacramental, if not high church. Evangelism is carried out in an extremely low-key manner, readily discerned in the denomination's major radio program, "The Lutheran Hour." The use of alcohol and tobacco is common throughout the synod.

Although the LCMS was indeed spared from the encroachment of liberalism during the fundamentalist–modernist dispute, the influence of biblical criticism within the denomination has been more and more apparent with the passage of time. In 1969 Jacob A. O. Preus was elected president of the Missouri Synod. A staunch theological conservative, Preus was disturbed by what he saw as an increasingly dominant liberalizing theology at Concordia Seminary in St. Louis. Therefore, in January 1974 the complicated, scrappy, but brilliant church executive suspended the school's moderate president, John Tietjen. This action immediately produced a strike of Concordia faculty and students who were sympathetic with Tietjen, resulting ultimately in their departure to form an opposition seminary—Concordia Seminary in Exile (Seminex.) By 1976 the general situation within the LCMS had worsened to the point that the church's moderate minority established a new denomination, the Association of Evangelical Lutheran Churches (AELC)—now more than 100,000 strong—supported in large measure by disenchanted Missouri Synod intellectuals and activists.

Apart from the behind-the-scenes politics associated with this civil war, the major theological issue at stake was biblical inerrancy. The conservative majority (bolstered in the wider evangelical movement by *Christianity Today* and LCMS theologian John Warwick Montgomery) insisted on inerrancy as a denominational standard; the moderates, mainly at Concordia Seminary in St. Louis, repudiated the concept. This struggle in the Missouri Synod can be viewed as a fight between the evangelical establishment within the denomination and the avant-garde evangelical left, the intellectual minority.[6]

Smaller Denominations

There are a large number of smaller distinctively evangelical denominations in the United States. Some of these, set up in the nineteenth (or early twentieth) century, stand squarely within the holiness and Arminian traditions. Prominent among them are the Christian and Missionary Alliance (founded in 1881 by A. B. Simpson, an ex-Presbyterian minister who focused his work on the masses of poor immigrants, skid-row alcoholics, prostitutes, and the like in New York City); the Free Methodist Church of North America (established in 1860 by B. T. Roberts, a strict Wesleyan who opposed the pew-rental system favoring the well-to-do introduced into the then Methodist Episcopal Church in 1852, and preferred "free seats" in all churches); The Wesleyan Church (organized in 1843 through the influence of Orange Scott, partly as a protest against the Methodist Episcopal Church's refusal to take an unflinching stand against slavery); and the Church of the Nazarene (formed in 1907 out of a group of rescue missions).[7]

Important distinctively evangelical denominations with a particular ethnic heritage include the Baptist General Conference (founded in 1852 by Swedish Baptists); the noncreedal Evangelical Covenant Church of America (established in 1885 by Swedish Lutheran pietists who stressed personal religious experience); the Evangelical Free Church of America (organized in 1884, also by Swedish pietists, and later joined by Norwegians and Danes as well); and the Christian Reformed Church (formed in 1857 by strict Dutch Calvinists).

Significant distinctively evangelical denominations formed as a result of the fundamentalist–modernist dispute and its aftermath include the Conservative Baptist Association (founded in 1947 by former American Baptists disgruntled by the trend toward liberalism in the American Baptist Churches, particularly in foreign mission work); the Conservative Congregational Christian Conference—the CCCCs (established originally in 1948 in opposition to the prospective merger of the Congregational Christian Churches and the Evangelical and Reformed Church into the United Church of Christ, which was consummated in 1959); the Orthodox Presbyterian Church (organized in 1936 as a protest against liberalizing tendencies in what is now The United Presbyterian Church in the U.S.A.); the Reformed Presbyterian Church, Evangelical Synod (formed in 1965); and the National Fellowship of Brethren Churches (set up in 1881–1883 by former members of the pacifist Church of the Brethren and eventually functionally divided into two distinctive wings of the same wider association—the Grace group, of Winona Lake, Indiana, which is more Calvinistic and congregational in government, and the Ashland, Ohio, group, which tends to be Arminian in theology).[8]

These denominations—a grouping that omits fundamentalist and pentecostal bodies—are all, generally speaking, good representatives of the evangelical center and right; though some of them, in their early days, stood farther to the left. Like The Lutheran Church–Missouri Synod and the Southern Baptist Convention, however, they too are beginning to feel the impact of the evangelical left, most notably the Evangelical Covenant Church of America, the Christian Reformed Church, the Baptist General Conference, the Conservative Baptist Association, The Wesleyan Church, the Free Methodist Church of North America, and the Brethren Church (Ashland group). In particular, the faculty of some of their seminaries continue slowly to move leftward on the evangelical spectrum in biblical studies, theology as a whole, broad cultural analysis, ecumenical stance, politics, and lifestyle. Prominent among these changing institutions of higher learning are North Park Theological Seminary, Chicago (Evangelical Covenant Church of America); Bethel Theological Seminary, St. Paul, Minnesota (Baptist General Conference); and Conservative Baptist Theological Seminary, Denver.

Although left-leaning academics, pastors, and laity of the aforementioned denominations often try to remain loyal members of their respective churches in order to facilitate reform from *within* ("subversives for Christ," I have termed them), many find the process too slow uncomfortable, and frustrating. As an alternative, some of them move to a more inclusive and ecumenical denomination of the same theological and ecclesiastical tradition, in which they do not have to worry constantly about heresy charges on the one hand and complaints about their lifestyles on the other. Thus Conservative Baptists may become American Baptists; Orthodox Presbyterians, United Presbyterians; Free Methodists, United Methodists; and so on. Others, however, may forsake their inherited traditions completely, moving from a conservative Calvinist church to a generally liberal Arminian body, or from a low-church denomination to one that stresses its catholicity, for instance. Of special note here is the increasing number of conservative Baptists and Plymouth Brethren (an extremely low-church fundamentalist group) who become high-church Episcopalians.

National Association of Evangelicals

The National Association of Evangelicals has been a major symbol of the evangelical right and center during the 60s and 70s. In 1929 J. Elwin Wright and others organized the New England Fellowship, made up of evangelicals from many denominations. This group had a strong concern for a national fellowship of evangelicals, which was realized in April 1942 with the founding of the NAE in St. Louis. The NAE, whose headquarters are located in Wheaton, Illinois (the "holy city" of evangelicals), is a voluntary association of evangelical denominations, churches, schools, organizations, and individuals, established as an alternative to the ecumenical and predominantly liberal National Council of Churches (NCC). The National Association of Evangelicals is also a fellowship with a strong creedal stance. Its statement of faith begins with a clause focusing on biblical authority: "We believe the Bible to be the inspired, the only infallible, authoritative Word of God."

The NAE provides an evangelical identification for 30,000 churches and 3½ million Christians. At the present time it represents 35 complete denominations (including numerous holiness and pentecostal bodies and a few pacifist groups) and individual churches from 30 other denominations (some of them having an affiliation with the NCC as well).

Resolutions passed by the NAE at its annual conventions have been uniformly conservative, as might well be expected. These have included expressions *against* television permissiveness in programming, homosexual practice, abortion, and advertising of alcoholic beverages; and *for* local action against pornography and for capital punishment. (On the advice of Dean M. Kelley, the NCC's director for civil and religious liberty and author of *Why Conservative Churches Are Growing,* Henry Schwarzchild of the American Civil Liberties Union invited the NAE to join its National Coalition Against the Death Penalty. Of course the NAE declined the invitation on "biblical grounds." The correspondence between Schwarzchild and Floyd Robertson of the NAE, recently published in *Christianity and Crisis* (February 21, 1977, pp. 30–32), is fascinating in that it provides a good example of two "biblical" arguments on the subject. Schwarzchild, however, believes that the NAE's position rests more firmly on concepts of civil justice and social effect than on Scripture.)

The National Association of Evangelicals has a number of commissions and affiliates. Its Office of Public Affairs in Washington, D.C., headed by Floyd Robertson, works to correct any infringement of religious liberty. The Evangelical Foreign Missions Association, the foreign mission arm of the NAE, is the largest in the world, with over 70 member mission boards comprising 8500 missionaries serving in almost every part of the world. The NAE's National Association of Christian Schools functions to promote private Christian day schools as an alternative to public education at that level. The National Religious Broadcasters (NRB), with over 650 member stations, program producers, and associates, seeks to effect religious freedom in broadcasting, guided by an established code of ethics for evangelical broadcasting.

The NAE's Commission on Chaplains acts as a processing agency for NAE member denominations in placing chaplains with the armed forces. Its Commission on Higher Education, composed of presidents of

NAE–related Bible institutes, colleges, and seminaries, probes common problems of higher education today—financing, governmental relations, and legislation, to name a few. The Evangelical Churchmen Commission and the Women's Fellowship Commission encourage lay ministries. The Evangelical Home Missions Association's interest include lay witness, spiritual renewal, church planting, and work among immigrants, poor communities, prisoners, and foreign-language groups. The NAE also has a Stewardship Commission and a very impressive World Relief Commission that supplements emergency relief in time of war and natural disaster with long-range self-help rehabilitation programs.

The influence of the evangelical left on the NAE is gradually being felt, partly through its Evangelical Social Action Commission, made up largely of the NAE's almost invisible Democrats, pacifists, and minority members. This commission, which has not yet been able to affect the NAE's major resolutions, serves as a medium for education on social needs and encourages the application of biblical principles to prominent contemporary social issues.

Although the National Association of Evangelicals remains a bastion of social, economic, and political conservatism, the situation may be slowly changing, as evidenced by the recent revitalization of the Evangelical Social Action Commission, leftward trends at NAE-related colleges and seminaries, and some of the major speakers from the evangelical left who were invited to the NAE's 35th annual convention in February 1977. Included among the latter were David Hubbard, president of Fuller Seminary; Bill Leslie, pastor of Chicago's LaSalle Street Church; Donn Moomaw, pastor of Bel Air Presbyterian Church in Los Angeles; Bernard Ramm, formerly professor of theology at Eastern Baptist Theological Seminary in Philadelphia; and Ronald J. Sider, former chairperson of Evangelicals for Social Action and author of *Rich Christians in an Age of Hunger*. A change of significant proportions could be emerging within the NAE, but few people are holding their breath in anticipation of that possibility.

EVANGELICAL CAUCUSES IN MAINLINE DENOMINATIONS

Many evangelicals, probably an increasing number overall, are now members of congregations and parishes affiliated with the historic Protestant denominations, the leadership of which became predominantly liberal after the fundamentalist–modernist dispute. (A *liberal* in this context means, simply, a nonevangelical—a person who does not have a firm commitment to the full authority of Scripture, the need for conversion to Christ, and the mandate for evangelism.)

With continued upward social mobility, a large number of evangelicals have found themselves more comfortable in "respectable" or mainline denominations (identifying themselves as United Presbyterians or Episcopalians, for example) than in those designated *sectarian* by the wider society. Indeed, sectarian churches have not generally been popular with the upper middle class, and there is a strong tendency in modern Western society to avoid creating boundaries of any kind, especially rigid boundaries, that would exclude people (a fact clearly relevant to religious organizations). In addition, many evangelicals today would rather work for reform and renewal along biblical lines *within* a largely liberal denomination than criticize it as apostate from the outside.

Evangelicals are well aware of their numbers and visibility in all the historic denominations. In view of this fact, they have begun to take the political nature of denominational bureaucracies seriously, recognizing that their own concerns will not be actively considered by the established liberal leadership unless there is good reason—unless a large number of evangelical clergy and laity *demand* to be heard by and represented within that leadership, and make such recognition the requirement for their continued financial support of denominational programs. In other words, no taxation without representation. Obviously, the major concerns of evangelicals in these denominations center on the hope that the denominational leadership itself will ultimately reaffirm biblical authority and the church's evangelistic task in both its national and its world mission.

In order to gain enfranchisement within the historic denominations, evangelicals have begun to form caucuses or advocacy groups similar to those organized in recent years by ethnic minorities and women to effect change and guarantee their recognition by the denominational hierarchies. These groups are proliferating and growing in numbers and are far more political and activist in character than their charismatic counterparts in the same denominations. (The latter are generally content to gather for fellowship alone rather than for advocacy.) Thus the evangelical organizations are more controversial and threatening to the denominational leadership than are the charismatic fellowships. The most important among these advocacy groups have been formed in The United Presbyterian Church in the U.S.A., The United Methodist Church, and The Episcopal Church.

Presbyterian Lay Committee and Presbyterians United for Biblical Concerns

The Presbyterian Lay Committee was incorporated in 1965 as an independent organization of United Presbyterian laity that reports annually to the General Assembly of the denomination. At its inception, the Lay Committee was particularly concerned about "the increasing emphasis of the Church on social and political action and the lessening emphasis on providing spiritual leadership as a Christian, Bible-believing institution."

The present objectives of the Presbyterian Lay Committee are five in number. First, the organization wants to see a greater stress on the teaching of Scripture as "the authoritative Word of God" in United Presbyterian seminaries and churches. Second, it seeks to emphasize "the need for presenting Jesus Christ the Redeemer through preaching, teaching, and witnessing with evangelical zeal, as the primary mission of the Church." The Lay Committee is strongly interested in evangelism, regular Bible study, and prayer. Third, it encourages individual ministers and laity to become involved in social, economic, and political affairs as Christian citizens. But, fourth, the Lay Committee discourages the larger church bodies (the General Assembly, for instance) from "issuing pronouncements or taking actions unless the authority to speak and act is clearly Biblical, the competence of the church body has been established, and all viewpoints have been thoroughly considered." Fifth, it seeks to provide United Presbyterians with a regular source of information on significant issues facing the church. To do this it employs a staff of field directors to nurture the more than 60 chapters of the Lay Committee and, more importantly, it publishes a monthly newspaper, *The Presbyterian Layman* (over 300,000 circulation), sent free to all ordained United Presbyterian ministers and interested laity.

The Lay Committee is supported by over 20,000 contributors, most of whom give less than $25 annually. It has a board of directors made up of United Presbyterian lay men and women and a salaried professional staff of four individuals based at headquarters in Philadelphia.

Although the Presbyterian Lay Committee was begun by a group of politically conservative evangelicals opposed to liberalizing trends, both theological and political, in the denomination, it has become slightly more moderate over the years. The *Layman,* incidentally, is the best and most interesting single source of news available on what is happening in The United Presbyterian Church in the U.S.A.

Presbyterians United for Biblical Concerns (PUBC) was organized in 1965 to offer substantive amendments to the then controversial proposed "Confession of 1967," which, with other historic confessions of the church (including the Westminster), has now become part of the denomination's Book of Confessions. Many of PUBC's suggestions, giving the proposed Confession of 1967 a more conservative character, were incorporated in the final draft.

Unlike the Lay Committee, PUBC is composed of both laity and clergy. It, too, has a board of directors and publishes a journal, *Presbyterian Communique,* which comes out less regularly than the *Layman.* The organization's statement of purpose reflects a clearly biblical, evangelical, and very Reformed (Calvinistic) position. In terms of its general stance and leadership, PUBC is probably more moderate and ecumenical than the Lay Committee. It stresses the need for evangelism and biblical social action by sponsoring conferences and consultations (and occasional position papers) for clergy and laity alike. At each General Assembly PUBC hosts a breakfast for commissioners and visitors. The speakers at these events have included notables of the evangelical left including John MacKay, president emeritus of Princeton Theological Seminary; black evangelist Tom Skinner; former Senator Harold Hughes (Democrat–Iowa); David Hubbard; and Senator Mark Hatfield (Republican–Oregon).

PUBC sees itself as "a fellowship of evangelical Presbyterians who love Christ" and a group of Christians who are "committed to His Body, the Church." Supported by membership enrollments and other contributions, its headquarters are located in Oakland, California. PUBC is "a theologically-oriented fellowship, which understands the value of active involvement and, where necessary, creative dissent within The United Presbyterian Church in the United States of America." If the Lay Committee is dedicated first and foremost to church *order,* PUBC is probably more keenly interested in church *renewal.* Despite differences in style and emphasis, however, both organizations have very similar concerns and do cooperate with each other.

Good News

Good News, or the Forum for Scriptural Christianity, is an evangelical advocacy movement and fellowship within The United Methodist Church. Its origins go back to July 1966, when the *New Christian Advocate,* the official ministers' magazine of The Methodist Church, published an article by Charles W. Keysor entitled ''Methodism's Silent Minority,'' written in response to the editor's invitation to write about the beliefs of Methodist evangelicals. Keysor received several hundred letters from Methodists across the country saying, in effect, ''I didn't know anybody else believed as I do.'' Orthodox Methodists, having lost control of their denomination, had become isolated from each other. They had no common voice and virtually no denominational impact. Thus a group of committed evangelicals organized Good News in 1967 to provide a point of cohesion as a movement of theological conservatives in what is now The United Methodist Church.

Good News, based in Wilmore, Kentucky, is governed by a board of directors made up of United Methodist clergy and laity. The first issue of its magazine, also called *Good News* and edited by Keysor, appeared in March 1967 with an unpaid circulation of about 5500. By the end of 1976, the bimonthly had a paid circulation of 15,000 in 50 states and 35 foreign countries. Because of its controversial conservative theological (and sometimes cultural) views, *Good News* has met with considerable opposition from denominational leaders at various levels.

As a somewhat underground movement within The United Methodist Church, Good News seeks to encourage the denomination to awaken to its responsibility to enfranchise and minister effectively to the large and growing number of orthodox Christians within its ranks. National and regional meetings are held on a regular basis, with attendance sometimes reaching nearly 3000.

The United Methodist Church is organized into 73 annual conferences, or regional units. At the end of 1976, Good News–aligned renewal groups had been formed or were forming in 52 annual conferences. These groups engage in Bible study and teaching, conduct summer camps, and work politically to elect evangelical delegates to various offices in the church structures at all levels.

Good News operates with a small, salaried staff. Its budget, raised completely by contributions from individual United Methodists, was only $9813 in 1967; by 1977 it had grown to $372,718. The movement publishes its own series for membership confirmation and training of youth in evangelical Christianity, *We Believe*. This series is often used by evangelical United Methodist pastors as an alternative to the official denominational publications dealing with the same issues.

Disenchanted with what it views as secularized teaching at denominational seminaries, Good News is presently considering the possibility of establishing a new, distinctively evangelical United Methodist school of theology for evangelically minded prospective clergy (Asbury Theological Seminary, Wilmore, Kentucky, an independent Wesleyan school, meets this need right now).

Theologically, Good News stands squarely in the tradition of Wesleyan, Arminian orthodoxy, which has never been quite so rigid doctrinally as its Calvinist counterpart. On July 20, 1975, the statement, "An Affirmation of Scriptural Christianity for United Methodists," was adopted by the Good News board of directors at Lake Junaluska, North Carolina. The "Junaluska Affirmation" is quite brief, professing a traditional trinitarian theology, the sinfulness of men and women, salvation through faith in Christ alone, the need for sanctification, the importance of the institutional church, the authority of Scripture ("the guide and final authority for the faith and conduct of individuals and the doctrines and life of the church"), and the necessity of "good works" as the evidence of a living faith. The conclusion of this statement of orthodox Methodism is highly significant, because it is fully consistent with the social holiness demanded by John Wesley and inherent in the whole Wesleyan tradition, and it demonstrates the degree to which the evangelical left has influenced Good News:

> Our life in Christ includes an unstinting devotion to deeds of kindness and mercy and a wholehearted participation in collective efforts to alleviate need and suffering. The believer will work for honesty, justice and equity in human affairs; all of which witness to inherent rights and a basic dignity common to all persons created in the image of God. . . . Thus, we remember that faith without works is dead.

The Fellowship of Witness

The Fellowship of Witness is a movement within The Episcopal Church. Organized in 1965, it has held national and regional conferences nearly every year since then. Its informal newsletter has grown to a full-scale magazine, *Kerygma,* published quarterly. The Fellowship of

Witness has also given birth to the Trinity Episcopal School for Ministry in Pittsburgh, which opened its doors to students in 1976.

Members of The Fellowship of Witness are concerned about the dramatic decline in communicants of The Episcopal Church over the last several years. They believe that this decline is primarily the result of a loss of authority in the church; an authority, the fellowship feels, grounded in "faithfulness to the Holy Scriptures, the certain word of God to Christians." It accuses The Episcopal Church of responding to the urgencies of the moment with a pragmatic or emotional reaction rather than standing firmly on the truths of the Bible and acting accordingly from that foundation. The fellowship dislikes the church's use of "demythologized object lessons" (you don't have to believe it really happened), "existential relativism" (each person finds his or her own truth), and "situation ethics" (as long as you think it is loving, go ahead and do it).

Members of The Fellowship of Witness long to see The Episcopal Church return to the authority of Scripture as interpreted by the ecumenical creeds and the Thirty-nine Articles of Anglicanism. To makes its beliefs known, it acts as a fellowship and advocacy group for evangelicals within the church. Unlike the United Presbyterian and United Methodist evangelical caucuses, The Fellowship of Witness is part of a larger international movement, the Evangelical Fellowship in the Anglican Communion, founded in 1961, with 21 group members in North and South America, Great Britain, Africa, Asia, and Australasia, and individual members in about 2c other countries.

The concrete goals of the fellowship, which is governed by a board of directors made up of clergy and laity and supported by membership enrollments and individual contributions, include an intention to: (1) foster fellowship among Anglican evangelicals throughout the world; (2) federate regional evangelical Episcopal fellowships where none exist; (3) "bear witness with courage and charity to the great Biblical and Reformation principles throughout the Anglican Communion"; (4) formulate policy in matters of common concern (advocacy); and (5) exchange news.

The real influence of the Presbyterian Lay Committee, Presbyterians United for Biblical Concerns, Good News, and The Fellowship of Witness is hard to determine at this time. Members of these groups declare that their influence is substantial and growing; liberal opponents in the respective denominations say not. We can be quite certain, however, that the continued growth in numbers of individual evangelicals within the historic (and still predominantly liberal) denominations will enhance the attractiveness of such movements. At any rate, they are now a force that denominational hierarchies will have to reckon with, whether they like it or not.

Although the evangelical left has indeed influenced these denominational renewal groups, the organizations themselves still bear the marks of the evangelical center and right. The Fellowship of Witness, Good News, PUBC, and the Presbyterian Lay Committee all were born in the turbulent mid-60s and reacted against the left social activism of their parent denominations at that time. For many of the founding members, conservative politics and cultural attitudes—so it seems—characterized their goals nearly as much as did conservative theology. And, despite the fact that this initial cultural and political conservatism has been moderated in recent years, and despite some of their official statements affirming a strong commitment to social justice and peace, these organizations are better known for what they *oppose* than what they affirm. It is quite possible, moreover, that evangelical caucuses would be more welcome and influential within the historic denominations if they were to commit themselves, visibly and actively, to peace and social justice to the same degree that they pursue spiritual renewal. After all, faith without works *is* dead.

In a word, the theology and church life of the evangelical right and center is marked, in general, by traditional, but not extreme, cultural conservatism. It is also characterized by growth, vitality, and a faith commitment that goes beyond mere words all the way to the pocketbook. Liberals in the historic denominations who ignore or complain about the numerical success of evangelical churches and ministries had better take a hard look at the current demise of their own ministries and churches, and ask why.

5

Evangelism

In Protestant liberal, Roman Catholic, and secular circles, the words *evangelical* and *evangelism* are often used incorrectly to mean the same thing (i.e., evangelical equals evangelistic). Both are derived from the same Greek root, *euangelion,* the good news. However, evangelical is something you *are,* evangelism is something you *do.* For evangelicals, evangelism is the active proclamation and demonstration of the good news that Jesus Christ came into the world to save sinners from the consequences of their sin, to make them whole, to reconcile them to God. God created man and woman in his own image to have fellowship with him. But we chose to rebel against God. Being estranged from God, yet responsible to him, we thus became subject to divine wrath. Sin is disobedience to God, and we are all sinners. Jesus Christ, God's eternal Son, is the only mediator between us and God. Born of Mary, he fulfilled our humanity in a life of perfect obedience to God. By his death in our place, he revealed the divine love and upheld divine justice, making possible our reconciliation with God (the substitutionary atonement). In Christ, God has granted us a pardon for our sins. But to be effective a pardon must be accepted. Our acceptance of God's gracious pardon by faith in Jesus Christ through an act of the will is an acknowledgment that we are indeed sinners in need of salvation, that we believe the Gospel and repent of our sins (for evangelicals, there is no *salvific* merit in good works apart from faith). God, then, forgives us, blots out our sins, remembers them no longer, and makes us "new creatures in Christ." In a spiritual sense, we are born again.

For most center and right evangelicals, all men and women are either saved or lost, bound for either eternal life in God's presence (heaven) or eternal separation from him (hell). There is simply no in-between possibility, since Christ is the one way to God. Basing their understanding of salvation and the evangelistic task primarily on the Gospel of John and the Pauline epistles, right and center evangelicals make evangelism their first priority. They see it as the number-one task of Christians individually and the church collectively. For them the process of making converts is simple. The unconverted are told the Gospel story from Scripture, and they may either accept it or reject it. Center and right evangelicals usually also believe that ignorance of the Gospel is no excuse. The heathen are lost just as much as those who have heard the good news but have rejected it. This situation, obviously, adds urgency to the evangelistic task.

For right and center evangelicals, conversion is focused on a personal experience of God in Jesus Christ—despite the rational belief systems formulated and required by their theologians. This experience itself may be dramatic and profound, as it was with Paul and Martin Luther, or it may be quiet and subdued, as it was with John Calvin and John Wesley. But there is never any doubt that it actually happened, and, more often than not, a born-again believer can state the time and place of his or her "second birth." The evangelical understanding of evangelism, moreover, has not generally been oriented to the institutional church, its tradition and sacraments. Nor is it ipso facto related to the practice of good deeds. It is not primarily church membership recruitment (as in Protestant liberalism), nor is it social action (as in the secular Christianity of the 60s). For the most part, center and right evangelicals insist that church membership comes *after* conversion (the true church being the invisible body of believers), and social action (good works) comes as a result of the new birth, not as part of the process of salvation. Only new people can create a new society. Finally, evangelicals as a whole see evangelism as the task of all Christians, not just of religious professionals; however, they do recognize that some believers have the *gift* of evangelism, a special divine calling to the evangelistic task. Among these, Billy Graham, of course, is acknowledged as the greatest of all in modern times.

Born in 1918, Billy Graham is now near the end of his professional ministry as the world's most eminent evangelist. Graham's rise to fame, as we saw earlier, began in a revival tent with a "sawdust trail" in Los Angeles in 1949. But no tent could long hold the vast numbers of sinners and saints who would come to hear him, and the evangelist soon moved his crusades to huge arenas in the major cities of the world. (Modern revivalism has appropriated a great deal of military language to get its message across. Thus we have crusades, campaigns, retreats, advances, rallies, and the like.)

In the wake of his early evangelistic successes, Graham launched his weekly "Hour of Decision" radio broadcasts and organized the Billy Graham Evangelistic Association, with a board of directors, in Minneapolis in 1950, complete with a full range of media efforts, including his monthly *Decision* magazine (circulated to millions around the world) and television specials and a staff of associate evangelists who joined his work in the years following. Aided by a ruggedly handsome appearance, a persuasive, charismatic personality, and an ecumenical spirit, Graham quickly became friend and chaplain to the rich and powerful, presidents, kings, and queens, though he never lost touch with the common people who represent his own roots.

Billy Graham did not attend theological seminary. He preaches a simple message, calling men and women everywhere to repent and believe the Gospel. Untold thousands of sinners have walked down the aisle in his crusades, responding to that call; more than a few have become highly committed Christian leaders of the first order. Graham's critics, as sincere and truthful as they may be, must contend with that fact.

But Graham, still one of the most admired of all Americans, cannot forever represent the last word in evangelism. Times and circumstances change, and so do people. With the almost universal availability of television and other comparable electronic and printed media, mass evangelism is on the decline in the United States, and many (if not most) of those who attend the Graham crusades are born-again believers already. The evangelist's health is failing, moreover, and his close friendship with and support of Richard Nixon during the Watergate era has cost him dearly, despite his public repentance of that involvement.[1]

The rapid and profound cultural change that characterizes our time has had its effect even on evangelism. Graham's political conservatism has made him very unpopular with many theological liberals and with an increasing number of evangelicals too, particularly those on the left, who criticize his style and tactics as well. These Christians cannot accept his assertion that new people can be relied on to build a new society. Empirical evidence and the social struggles of the 60s demonstrate the falsehood of that assumption. Indeed, evangelism in the future will probably have to take on a more *holistic* approach. It will have to be concerned just as much with a person's physical, intellectual, and social well-being as with his or her spiritual condition. Graham's brother-in-law and heir apparent, Leighton Ford, is trying to address all those needs in his own evangelistic efforts.

Yet no one, not even his heir apparent, can succeed Graham; there can be no successor to that kind of charismatic leader. With Billy Graham's retirement or death, the whole character of mass evangelism may undergo a metamorphosis, or die completely. Already the famous evangelist, once the chief symbol of the evangelical center and right, the evangelical establishment, has been replaced by a politician, Jimmy Carter. Graham's influence as an evangelical was measured largely by his closeness, his personal access, to power in presidents and world leaders. He, like no other evangelical, could prevail upon the great and powerful to govern with righteousness (obviously he failed with Nixon). But Carter, already the most powerful world leader in his own right, is himself capable of exercising that power for the sake of righteousness. Both in the eyes of the evangelicals themselves and in the eyes of the public at large, Jimmy Carter is now "Mr. Evangelical."

CAMPUS CRUSADE FOR CHRIST

Begun in 1951 as a ministry to students at UCLA, Campus Crusade for Christ International was founded by ex-businessman Bill Bright and his wife, Vonette, with the help and encouragement of the late Wilbur M. Smith, then teaching at Fuller Seminary, and the late Henrietta Mears, then director of Christian education at the First Presbyterian Church of Hollywood, California (Bright regards Mears as his spiritual mother).

Crusade's headquarters are located at Arrowhead Springs, near San Bernardino, California, where the Brights attend a liberal United Presbyterian congregation. The ministry's multi-million-dollar administrative offices and guest accommodations are in what was formerly a luxury resort hotel in the San Bernardino mountains. Hundreds of Crusade's staff members work at the extremely well run headquarters in the coordination of recruitment and placement of all staff, administration and control of all financial operations, and production and marketing of mass media tools.

Campus Crusade is now an international organization, with over 5300 staff members working in 84 different countries. It is divided into a number of distinctive specialized ministries. Crusade's campus ministry program is probably the largest of its kind anywhere. Campus ministers, all of whom are college or university graduates (few attended seminary), conduct weekly training meetings; set up evangelistic outreaches; participate in Bible-study and prayer groups; and work with faculty, civic leaders, pastors, and local churches. In its lay ministry program, Crusade staff members work personally with pastors and church leaders to develop strategies for saturating entire communities and cities with the Gospel message. They also conduct lay training institutes and pastors' conferences. Crusade's high school ministry carries on its work through school administrations and youth leaders in local churches.

Other ministries developed by Campus Crusade for Christ include an international outreach to train nationals to evangelize their own countries; a ministry to the military; the Agape movement (a two-year "Christian Peace Corps" program); Athletes in Action (the staff of which, both amateurs and professionals in six sports, play some of the country's top university and college teams); and an international student ministry to the thousands of internationals studying and working in the United States and Canada.

Crusade also has a special prayer ministry (The Great Commission Prayer Crusade, headed by Vonette Bright); a prison ministry, in which staff assist chaplains, coordinate the outreach of lay volunteers into penal institutions, and assist parolees and their families in adjusting to society after release; a camping program; a music ministry, with groups performing in churches, civic organizations, military installations, prisons, high schools, colleges, and universities throughout the United States and the world; and an intercultural ministry designed to train minority men and women—Native Americans, Hispanic Americans, Asian Americans, and Afro-Americans—to reach their own people with the Gospel. This intercultural ministry is probably Crusade's most creative, and the one most concerned with social justice issues.

Bill Bright and Campus Crusade have become highly visible and very controversial in recent years. The evangelical left has linked Bright's Christian Embassy in Washington, D.C. (founded as a center for evangelism and spiritual renewal in the political community there) and his Here's Life, America! or I Found It! campaign to a right-wing "plot" to save America from liberalism and communism.[2] Here's Life, inaugurated in Atlanta in 1975, has been a program of evangelism to saturate major American cities and other urban centers of the world with the Gospel message during 1976–1977 and beyond. Crusade staff members, working together with sympathetic chruches in each city, organized this evangelistic thrust with thousands of volunteers making telephone calls and personal visits, and a full-scale media campaign using television, radio, and newspaper ads, billboards, buttons, and bumper stickers.

Campus Crusade for Christ emphasizes in all its ministries what it terms *aggressive evangelism*. Central to Crusade's message are the Four Spiritual Laws, developed by Bill Bright and contained in a widely distributed booklet first published in 1965.[3] These laws stress: (1) God's love and his plan for all people; (2) the sinfulness of men and women and their natural alienation from God; (3) the possibility of reconciliation with God through Christ; (4) and the need for a personal faith in Christ for salvation. The method of aggressive evangelism is simple. A staff worker—or anybody else, for that matter—presents the Four Spiritual Laws to a potential convert, using the Bible for reference. The latter is immediately invited to "receive Christ" through a sincere prayer of commitment. If he or she decides affirmatively, the new convert is encouraged to enroll in a follow-up program of discipleship, to join a church, and to learn to share his or her faith with others. Many critics argue that Crusade's methods are too rash, too anti-intellectual, too simplistic. Theologians often complain that the message is too narrow and without a solid theological content. Others feel that Crusade—led by Bright, the political conservative—neglects the social dimension of the Gospel entirely. But numbers count for Campus Crusade.

Although Campus Crusade for Christ is a well-financed organization for ministry, its staff members, including Bright himself, live very modestly. Each worker must raise his or her own support. Basic living allowances for a beginning staff member are $365 per month for a single person and $660 for a married couple (both of whom must be engaged in the ministry full-time). Housing, auto allowance, insurance, pension fund, and dependent children allowances are added to the basic stipend, but the money for these extras must be raised. According to the December 15, 1976 listing of nonprofit organizations, Crusade met the standards for charitable solicitation purposes of the Council of Better Business Bureaus. Included in this evaluation are some 40 guidelines that require of each group a responsible governing body, financial accountability, ethical fund raising, and truthful advertising and information. (Christian organizations that failed to meet the Council's standards include the Billy Graham Evangelistic Association and the Oral Roberts Association.)[4]

An approximately equal number of men and women are employed as Crusade staff members. And Crusade may have more women in full-time ministry than any other Protestant organization.

The success of Campus Crusade for Christ can probably be measured best in terms of converts to Christ rather than in terms of new church members. By May 1977 at least 60 percent of the American population had been exposed to Crusade's Here's Life, America! campaign, held in 165 cities across the country. According to its own estimates, more than 2 million phone callers responded to the number advertised through billboards, radio, television, and newspapers. Moreover, close to 7 million personal contacts were made, and nearly 550,000 people expressed a desire to "accept Christ."

But a statistical analysis of 400 churches in two Here's Life cities, Indianapolis, and Fresno, California, suggests that the massive evangelistic thrust was quite ineffective in terms of actual church growth. The survey, conducted by Win Arn of the Institute of American Church Growth in Arcadia, California, shows that 31 percent of the churches in the two cities participated in the program; about 29,000 phone calls were made; almost 6000 people had the Four Spiritual Laws explained to them; 1665 made a "decision for Christ." However, only 101 individuals completed Crusade's follow-up Bible-study program; and only 55 people became members of a church because of Here's Life (of the 55, 23 had had some kind of previous church involvement).

All this notwithstanding, Arn does speak appreciatively of the Here's Life campaign in general. He feels that *something,* at least, is being done here; it is the best evangelistic effort of Crusade to date, its evangelism has moved closer to the local church, laity are being trained and involved, and high visibility is being achieved.[5]

LAUSANNE '74

Evangelicals of the center and right have long been unhappy about the failure of the World Council of Churches (WCC) and the ecumenical movement as a whole to implement what they feel is the biblical mandate to evangelize the world. These evangelicals have seen in that movement, and in the WCC, in particular, a dominant trend toward syncretism, universalism, and a de-emphasis of evangelism that calls non-Christians to commit themselves to Christ. Indeed, evangelicals in general have viewed any belief in universal salvation as the enemy of a growing, vital church and its evangelistic task. If everyone is saved already, why bother with evangelism?

To reaffirm their belief in the mandate for world evangelization and to map a strategy to achieve it (in theory, at least), 2430 evangelical participants from 150 countries (and about 1500 observers and guests) gathered in Lausanne, Switzerland, in July 1974 for a ten-day International Congress on World Evangelism. The idea for this meeting was Billy Graham's originally, and he was honorary chairperson of the event.

The congress included Bible studies, major speeches (prepared and circulated beforehand), demonstrations of evangelistic methods, and consideration of various styles of evangelism appropriate to different cultures of the world. Although the 29-member planning committee, representing nearly a score of countries, did invite more than 1000 participants (not including missionaries) from the Third World, most of the people in attendance were conservative and Western in outlook, and fit squarely into the evangelical right and center. But there were a few notable exceptions as speakers and participants who represented the evangelical left.

Francis Schaeffer, in a major address, affirmed the literal fall of Adam and Eve, and insisted that biblical inerrancy is the evangelical watershed. Carl F. H. Henry (as usual) urged evangelicals to become involved in social action but criticized the socialist option and argued that Marxist proposals for utopia do not really, as claimed, overcome human alienation. Rather, said Henry, they perpetuate that alienation by substituting one preferred class for another and by ignoring the spiritual dimension of human life.

On the other side of the evangelical spectrum—the left—two Latin Americans argued against the neat separation of evangelism and social concern. Samuel Escobar, a Peruvian, then secretary of the Inter-Varsity Christian Fellowship of Canada (now living in Argentina as president of the Latin American Theological Fraternity), criticized American imperialism, under which the rich are getting richer and the poor poorer, and, in effect, expressed his preference for socialism over capitalism. René Padilla, associate general secretary of the International Fellowship of Evangelical Students in Buenos Aires, denounced the ''culture Christianity'' inherent in the American way of life as no less harmful to the cause of the Gospel than secular Christianity.

Other plenary speakers, including Graham, kept closer in their addresses to the traditional evangelical understanding of evangelism. (Malcolm Muggeridge was another exception, however.)

A continuing committee was formed to help implement the Lausanne Covenant, drafted during the congress by yet another committee, this one chaired by the conciliatory Anglican rector and exegete John R. W. Stott. The long statement, focusing on the evangelistic task, was signed by a majority of the official participants, including Billy Graham. It puts forward strongly worded statements on the authority and power of the Bible (''without error in all that it affirms,'' at the insistence of Schaeffer); the uniqueness and universality of Christ; the urgency of the evangelistic task; the return of Christ (''personally and visibly, in power and glory, to consummate his salvation and his judgment''); and Christian social responsibility (a section strengthened by pressure from the evangelical left),[6] affirming that

> evangelism and socio-political involvement are both part of our Christian duty. . . . The message of salvation implies also a message of judgment upon every form of alienation, oppression and discrimination, and we should not be afraid to denounce evil and injustice wherever they exist. . . . Faith without works is dead.[7]

The influence of Lausanne '74 was sufficiently great that it was felt even at the Fifth General Assembly of the World Council of Churches, which met in Nairobi in December 1975, and was reflected in the document entitled "Confessing Christ Today," formulated at that assembly, and reaffirming the WCC's commitment to evangelism.

THE CHURCH GROWTH MOVEMENT

Church growth, for center and right evangelicals, is the necessary and logical outgrowth of evangelism, properly understood. Given the evangelical boom in recent years, evangelical scholars, pastors, evangelists, and laity have been encouraged to put an even greater emphasis on church growth than in the past. In fact, it has become almost a science, with the result that numerous programs and institutes of church growth have been organized, some of them utilizing not only Scripture and theology as the basis for their work but the social and behavioral sciences as well.

"Evangelism Explosion" and James D. Kennedy

James D. Kennedy's Evangelism Explosion has been one of the most popular training programs in evangelism for laity in the local church. Except for its stress on and relationship to the local church, Evangelism Explosion, in content and method, is not significantly different from the general approach used by Campus Crusade for Christ.

Conceived by Kennedy, senior minister of Coral Ridge Presbyterian Church, Ft. Lauderdale, Florida, the program has been practiced in his church since the late 60s and has spread to hundreds, if not thousands, of congregations throughout the United States and abroad. Kennedy suggests that ministers who want their churches to grow should recruit several people from the congregation to learn and practice evangelism with the minister. At the end of a training program, these individuals (Kennedy started with four) enlist more, and so on, until a given congregation could have hundreds of people practicing evangelism methodically at the same time.

New workers are to be recruited by a personal visit. A trained participant in the program explains it briefly and then invites the prospective worker to a dinner, where a greater explanation of the goals and principles of the program is shared. Testimonies to what has already been accomplished are given here, and potential workers are asked to commit themselves for the entire 4½-month training program or else not start at all.

Kennedy offers three types of concrete training in evangelism. First, there is class instruction on the day the recruits come to the church for visitation and before they go out into the community. A brief lecture on the week's topic begins the session, and assignments are given for the following week. Then class members are divided into pairs to practice what they learned the previous week. Second, homework is given that focuses on portions of Scripture to be memorized and used in the course of "witnessing" during visitation. These are recited and checked each week in class. (Kennedy has prepared a detailed workbook, *Evangelism Explosion,* on how to present the Gospel "logically and interestingly.") Third, there is on-the-job training. Each trainee goes out with a trained worker and listens as this person endeavors to lead someone to Christ. Personal witnessing—giving "a simple, positive statement of the Good News of the Gospel"—is the style of evangelism central to the Kennedy program.

The schedule of visitation evangelism designed by Kennedy centers on two three-hour periods each week, one in the morning (for those whose jobs don't conflict) and one in the evening. After each of these periods, a report-back gathering is arranged to reduce dropouts and prevent people from being discouraged when they fail. Trainees are taught how to get "into" the Gospel themselves, how to find out where a person they intend to reach with the Gospel is spiritually, how to present the Gospel to that individual, and how to bring him or her to commitment in the end. Follow-up procedure includes several return visits, after which an attempt is made to get the new believer into a small Bible-study group of several mature Christians and four or five newer Christians.

Later, after the new convert has been taught how to study the Bible, to pray, and to "live the Christian life," he or she is encouraged to come into the evangelism program to learn how to share his or her faith with others. There is always an emphasis on "spiritual multiplication." And since the program is centered in the local church and is carried out by church laity, it is the local church itself that benefits in terms of growth. [8]

Fuller Evangelistic Association's Department of Church Growth and C. Peter Wagner

The high priest of the contemporary church growth movement is Donald McGavran, an eminent scholar of the Christian world mission (*missiology* is the word for that academic discipline) and a minister of the

Christian Church (Disciples of Christ). McGavran founded the Institute of Church Growth at Northwest Christian College, Eugene, Oregon, in 1961, and admitted one student. In 1965 he moved to Pasadena, California, as founding dean of Fuller Seminary's School of World Mission, established to provide professional missiological training for career missionaries of long-term standing and for overseas nationals who had risen to positions of leadership in their own churches. Currently, over 100 such people from a wide spectrum of denominations pass through the school each year.

The designation *church growth movement* emerged from the work of McGavran and his disciples—scholarship that brought together in a creative manner mission theology and the best results of social-scientific research, centering on cross-cultural studies. The research methodology and findings of the church growth movement began to be applied to North America only in 1972. Before that the focus had been almost entirely on Third World nations, especially where Christianity was taking root in new soil. Now church growth has become a significant field of study in post—M.Div. Doctor of Ministry (D.Min.) programs offered by seminaries and designed for the professional education of pastors and denominational executives in the United States.

At least four different organizations dedicated to providing training services or consultation on church growth have come into being since 1972—the Institute for American Church Growth, Arcadia, California; the National Church Growth Research Center, Washington, D.C.; Fuller Evangelistic Association's Department of Church Growth; and The Robert H. Schuller Institute for Successful Church Leadership, Garden Grove, California. Several denominational agencies and "parachurch" organizations (Campus Crusade and Evangelism Explosion, among them) have adopted the church growth methodology as their modus operandi, and the number is increasing.[9]

The Fuller Evangelistic Association itself was founded in 1943 by radio evangelist Charles Fuller, whose worldwide Sunday evening "Old Fashioned Revival Hour" broadcast made him America's best loved revivalist during the 40s, before Billy Graham. It was Fuller who was behind the establishment of Fuller Theological Seminary. After Fuller's death the "Old Fashioned Revival Hour" was renamed "The Joyful Sound," and took on a lower, more subdued profile, in keeping with the times. David Hubbard became its featured radio preacher. "The Joyful

Sound" continues to fulfill an evangelistic function; but more importantly, perhaps, it also provides a necessary vehicle to make Fuller Seminary visible to the multitudes of conservative evangelicals who listen to
the broadcast and read its monthly newspaper, *Today's Christian*. Contributions from such people keep the seminary in business.

C. Peter Wagner, former missionary to Latin America; student and
disciple of Donald McGavran; author of numerous books on world mission, evangelism, and church growth; and associate editor of the important bimonthly *Church Growth Bulletin* (Santa Clara, California), is an
officer of the Fuller Evangelistic Association and teaches in the School of
World Mission at Fuller Seminary. Wagner organized the association's
Department of Church Growth in 1976 to promote the concepts and
insights of the church growth movement throughout North America, to
offer professional church growth consultant services, and to develop new
and practical approaches to evangelism more generally. It does this work
primarily through teaching and preaching, one-day workshops for pastors
and lay leaders, high-intensity church growth seminars, and the publication and distribution of study–training packs for ministers.

C. Peter Wagner himself is a member of the largest and fastest growing
Congregational church in the United States, Lake Avenue Congregational Church (CCCC), Pasadena, California. Next to Robert H. Schuller
and Donald McGavran, now semi-retired, Wagner is the most important
motivator of church growth in America today.

The Robert H. Schuller Institute for Successful Church Leadership

A minister of the Reformed Church in America (RCA), Robert H.
Schuller does not fit neatly into the evangelical center and right designation. He is a rather nontheological disciple of Norman Vincent Peale
(another RCA minister) and his psychologically informed and success-
oriented *power of positive thinking*. (Schuller's brand of this middle-class
"theology" is termed *possibility thinking,* and he has authored a number
of popular books on the topic.)

On the one hand, many conservative evangelicals question whether
Schuller is really an evangelical at all. He avoids even talking about the
finer points of doctrine (and some of the not-so-fine points as well), and
shuns like the plague all controversial themes in his preaching, be they
theological or political. Schuller is extremely difficult to pin down. On
the other hand, evangelicals of the left and some Protestant liberals

criticize Schuller's stress on numbers rather than faithfulness to a Gospel, the "Way" of which is narrow and inherently unpopular, and his emphasis on bigger and better church buildings—both characteristic of what they feel are the worst priorities of the evangelical establishment. At present the Southern California pastor is planning a giant crystal cathedral in Garden Grove, estimated to cost no less than $14 million, and built to seat 4100 for services of worship and major cultural events.

Schuller started his church in Garden Grove in 1955, with no members and no money (few people at that time foresaw the way Orange County, where the church is located, would grow and flourish in the years following). The church itself was begun in a drive-in theater, and the success of that novel "drive-in ministry" was so great that numerous other pastors imitated the model. Today Schuller's church has over 8000 members and a very impressive and expansive campus. Furthermore, his visibility has been enhanced by the weekly telecast, "Hour of Power," originating at Garden Grove Community Church and seen coast to coast.

The Robert H. Schuller Institute for Successful Church Leadership was born out of Schuller's own success. General seminars on church growth are held several times a year on the church campus, and specialized conferences are also offered annually on church music, stewardship, "women's possibility thinkers," and ministry to singles (including never-marrieds and divorced people). Without a doubt Garden Grove Community Church has one of the best ministries to singles anywhere.

Schuller insists that his church growth conferences provide practical "how-to-do-it" exposure to programs for growth and success that can be adapted to a church of any size in any location. At each conference the Southern California pastor himself speaks five times on how to build successful churches now and also leads an hour-long session on church management. The church's staff members lead seminars and workshops on their individual specializations, including evangelism (door-to-door visitation that seeks to learn about the needs and "hurts" of local unchurched people); lay and clergy pastoral care; counseling; Christian education; stewardship; small-group fellowships; music; and special ministries to single adults, women, youth, and senior citizens. Clergy and laity of all denominations—from pentecostals to Unitarian–Universalists—attend the sessions where theological issues are generally ignored and sociological and psychological insights are stressed to the point that members of almost any denomination can get something of value from the week-long gathering. In fact, an increasing number of laity and clergy from liberal congregations attend the conferences, seeking practical help for their declining or dying churches. Even some of Schuller's severest critics have had their negative presuppositions "shot to hell" by attending the institute's programs.[10]

With the continued advance of secularization and the demise of so many denominations and individual congregations, we can safely predict that the church growth movement, aided by quite sophisticated theoreticians like McGavran and Wagner, and successful and persuasive pastors like Schuller and Kennedy, is here to stay.

"SPIRITUAL COUNTERFEITS" AND WALTER R. MARTIN

Among center and right evangelicals, any religious tradition that utilizes the writings and teachings of its own prophets as a supplement to the Scriptures is heretical. Likewise, all non-Christian traditions constitute false pathways to God, leading, ultimately, nowhere. They are cults in the most pejorative meaning of the word—*spiritual counterfeits* (a phrase coined in the Jesus movement)—to be exposed and fought against as part of the evangelistic task.

A number of contemporary evangelical scholars are engaged in this spiritual warfare, most of them from the right and center, a few from the left. Among the former are Anthony A. Hoekema, who teaches at Calvin Theological Seminary (Christian Reformed Church), Grand Rapids, Michigan; Gordon R. Lewis of Conservative Baptist Theological Seminary; and, most important of all, Walter R. Martin, who teaches at Melodyland School of Theology (charismatic) in Anaheim, California.

Martin, an ordained Southern Baptist minister and board member of Gordon-Conwell Theological Seminary, is the author of a dozen books on spiritual counterfeits, the most significant of which is *The Kingdom of The Cults,* regarded in evangelical circles as a classic study (with an axe to grind) of twenty mainline cults of our day including Mormonism, the Jehovah's Witnesses, Christian Science, and Unity. The author contributes regularly to such leading evangelical magazines as *Christianity Today, Eternity, Christian Life,* and *Action,* the official organ of the National Association of Evangelicals. He has appeared on numerous syndicated television and radio programs and has his own weekly half-hour radio broadcast, "Dateline Eternity," heard in California and Colorado.

Martin has also lectured on cults and Christian apologetics at hundreds of colleges, universities, and seminaries here and abroad.

Although Martin's work began single-handedly, it has expanded greatly through the Christian Research Institute (San Juan Capistrano, California), of which he is both founder and director. He now centers much of his effort on fighting "new religions" such as Krishna Consciousness, Transcendental Meditation, the Reverend Sun Myung Moon's Unification Church, the various rigidly authoritarian groups that emerged from the Jesus movement, and the occult. With the cooperation of scores of scholars, pastors, missionaries, and laity in Europe, Asia, and America, information on cults is forwarded to the institute for classification and use in research projects and storage in computer data systems.

The institute's library on cults, housed at Melodyland School of Theology, now numbers over 13,000 volumes. Research consultants keep abreast of contemporary trends and movements. With the help of a highly sophisticated information retrieval and processing system, the institute hopes eventually to supply Christian educational institutions throughout the world with the latest information about old and new cults.

The success of Martin and his colleagues in the fight against spiritual counterfeits is due largely to the mushrooming interest of the general public in modern cults—the Hare Krishnas and Moonies, most notably—and the controversies surrounding them, including the widespread practice of *deprograming*. Evangelicals and many others as well are willing to make substantial financial contributions to those who can and will expose and rescue their friends and children from these movements.

THE EVANGELICAL MEDIA

The evangelical center and right has taken full advantage of the American media explosion witnessed in recent years. Evangelical media efforts as a whole constitute one of the movement's biggest success stories. Television and radio programing, magazines, newspapers, book publishing, and cassette-type ministries have enabled evangelicals to get their message across to millions of unchurched Americans; and, more importantly perhaps, they have met the needs of the evangelicals themselves, providing them contact with their own leaders and national celebrities, a sense of identity with the larger evangelical (and charismatic) constituency, and spiritual nourishment for their lives. Indeed, we must emphasize here the contemporary viability of the persistence of a movement without coherent internal structure, hierarchy, or real membership, carried almost entirely by the mass media, without the need to bring people together for formal (business) purposes as distinct from expressive (fellowship and worship) ends. In a sense it is the evangelical media that identify and give visibility and content to the movement. In the beginning was the word, and the word became flesh. The medium is the message.

Evangelists—Charles Fuller, Kathryn Kuhlman, Billy Graham, Rex Humbard, and Oral Roberts, to name a few—have long made good use of television and radio. There are numerous local AM and FM radio stations and standard and UHF television stations that specialize in charismatic and evangelical programing. National Religious Broadcasters (Morristown, New Jersey) unites 650 individual broadcasts, national and international, large and small, and publishes its own bimonthly magazine, *Religious Broadcasting*. Most visible and significant are Pat Robertson's Christian Broadcasting Network (Portsmouth, Virginia), which produces a nightly variety and phone-in program, "The 700 Club," now available to about 70 percent of the television households in America on about 2000 cable television systems and over 100 radio stations; and former "700 Club" co-host Jim Bakker's PTL (Praise the Lord) Television Network (Matthews, North Carolina) and its PTL Club program, almost identical in style (and competitive with) Robertson's efforts. Both Bakker and Robertson are charismatics, and feature experience- and event-oriented talk shows with prominent Christian celebrities and vocal groups, supported entirely by the financial contributions of viewers. The programing is homey, Southern and Middle American, with men in double-knit suits and women in long dresses. Traditional religious and cultural values are emphasized, and "Christian rock" music is prominent on most of the programs.

The Christian Broadcasting Network (CBN) has been so successful that Pat Robertson is building an earth satellite transmission and receiving station (with the capability of transmitting the same telecast simultaneously in up to 32 languages) as part of the International Communications Center that CBN is constructing on a 142-acre site in Virginia Beach. The center will house television and radio production facilities, an international school of communications to train students from around the world in broadcasting, a conference facility, and a school of theology.[11] It is interesting to note that, for many evangelicals, Christian television programs have replaced the once mandatory Sunday and Wednesday evening services held by their churches.

Religious publishing, primarily evangelical and charismatic, has also experienced rapid growth during the 70s, so much so that *Publishers Weekly,* the secular book-trade journal, now puts out two special issues on religious books each year. Although the major focus of charismatic and evangelical book publishing is on devotional, sermonic, and how-to-do-it books, serious scholarship is not neglected. The most important evangelical book publishers (from right to left, roughly speaking) are Moody Press (Chicago); Fleming H. Revell (Old Tappan, New Jersey); Zondervan Publishing House (Grand Rapids, Michigan); William B. Eerdmans Publishing Company (Grand Rapids, Michigan); and Word Books (Waco, Texas)—a division of Word, Incorporated—recently bought by the American Broadcasting Company. Logos International (Plainfield, New Jersey) is the most significant publisher of charismatic titles. Some secular trade publishers, most notably Harper & Row and Doubleday, are also increasing their output of evangelical and charismatic books.

More than 2400 Christian bookstores (largely the very conservative Bible bookstores) are members of the Christian Booksellers Association (Colorado Springs). This organization holds an annual national convention and several regional miniconventions for publishers to introduce their forthcoming titles to CBA-affiliated book dealers. It also conducts a management training program for current and prospective book salespersons, and publishes its own monthly *Bookstore Journal* (one of two major evangelical book-trade journals, the other being *Christian Bookseller).* Charismatic and evangelical titles selling in the millions are not that uncommon. And distinctively evangelical Bible translations, including *The Living Bible* (Wheaton, Ill.: Tyndale House, 1971) and the *New American Standard Bible* (La Habra, Calif.: The Lockman Foundation, 1960), favorites of right and center evangelicals, do extremely well too.

Evangelical and charismatic magazines have enjoyed more visibility and increased circulation (a few in the hundreds of thousands) over the past decade or so. Prominent among mainstream evangelical journals are *Moody Monthly* (Chicago), a conservative family magazine; *Christianity Today* (Carol Stream, Illinois), the biweekly voice of the evangelical establishment, primarily for clergy and seminarians; *Eternity*

(Philadelphia), a monthly, less clergy oriented and somewhat to the left of *Christianity Today;* and *Christian Herald* (Chappaqua, New York), another family monthly, very moderate, almost mainline Protestant in its approach. Tyndale House's *The Christian Reader* (Wheaton, Illinois) is a quite conservative journal that follows the general format of *Reader's Digest* and is published every other month. Among distinctively charismatic magazines with a popular readership are the bimonthly *Logos Journal* (Plainfield, New Jersey); and *Christian life* (Wheaton, Illinois), a monthly edited by Robert Walker, who is sympathetic with the evangelical left in general and with evangelicals unjustly accused of heresy in particular (Walker felt the brunt himself when he became charismatic).

Also highly significant among evangelical media efforts is the Christian rock record and tape industry, a multi-million-dollar concern centered largely on ABC's Word, Incorporated. Most of that company's phenomenal financial success is derived from the sales of records and tapes made by Christian rock groups who perform in churches, on television, and in public concerts. The style of Christian rock, born in the Jesus movement, reflects the rhythms, dress, and highly sophisticated production that characterizes secular rock. But its lyrics are religious, it is "cleaner," and its recordings and tapes are rarely offered "on sale." Some Christian rock artists, André Crouch, and Love Song, for example, do very well indeed. In addition to music, cassette tapes of numerous evangelical and charismatic preachers and teachers are sold in Christian bookstores and by subscription. These cassette-type ministries are also on the rise.

Media and communications are indeed a major concern of the evangelical center and right. The proposed Billy Graham Center at Wheaton College (expected to cost at least $6 million) not only will house an institute of evangelism for Third World leaders; a lay Bible-training program; conferences; displays and exhibits; an evangelism and mission library; and the Billy Graham archives; it also will be the center of Wheaton College's Graduate School of Bible, Communications, and Missions, providing advanced training in television, satellite transmission of the Gospel, radio, journalism, and effective public speaking. Plans for the Billy Graham Center, as well as the greater plans of Pat Robertson and Oral Roberts, reflect the degree to which right and center evangelicals are now staking the future of their ministries on the electronic media.

6

Mainstream Evangelical Culture

In addition to blue-collar workers and farmers, a rapidly increasing number of business people, physicians, engineers, scientists, lawyers, politicians, athletes, entertainers, and other professionals are to be found in the ranks of center and right evangelicals. These men and women— celebrating upward social mobility and accommodating themselves more and more to the wider culture—see themselves as different from their non-Christian and nonevangelical colleagues and associates. In some ways they *are* different; in other ways they aren't.

Right and center evangelicals tend to be active church members, tithers, and political and cultural conservatives, whose close friends are almost always evangelicals too. They affirm traditional American role models and the nuclear family. Ideally, to be first-class Christians, men and women should marry and have children. The husband of course, is the breadwinner; the wife, as the resident domestic (though she may have a maid), stays home with the children and serves her husband, meeting his sexual needs. Men are considered to be the proper leaders of church and society, and most certainly head of the home. In marriage, the wife always must submit to her husband's will and authority in everything.

Center and right evangelicals are law-abiding citizens. They respect and firmly support "law and order," and are most often Republicans. Wealth, if acquired honestly, is approved—a concrete sign of God's blessing on a Christian family. The stereotyped successful evangelical of this variety is married (and has not been divorced), lives in a $150,000 home in an all-white suburb, is a businessman or physician, has two or three new cars, attends a big conservative evangelical church, is anti-evolution and antipornography, vacations in Europe or Hawaii, sends his children to a Christian college (or, increasingly, to a prestigious secular university), and does not drink, smoke, or gamble. The Husband reads *U.S. News and World Report* and, perhaps, *Business Week;* the Wife reads *Ladies' Home Journal* and *Good Housekeeping.* Both subscribe to *Moody Monthly* and Billy Graham's *Decision* magazine (*Logos Journal* and *Christian Life,* if they happen to be charismatic).

BUSINESSMEN'S ASSOCIATIONS

To help the right or center businessman or professional be a good Christian in his vocation as well as an effective witness for Christ, two large fellowship organizations exist (not unlike the Rotary and Kiwanis Clubs, to which many evangelicals also belong), one for evangelicals and one for charismatics. In recent years, there has also emerged a wide-spread interest in "Christian management techniques" for laity and clergy. The most popular trainers in this area are Ed Dayton and Ted Engstrom of World Vision International, who travel the country conducting workshops.

Center and right (mainly right) evangelicals have their own Christian Business Men's Committee U.S.A. (Glen Elyn, Illinois), founded in 1937, and made up of laymen who subscribe annually to a strict statement of doctrine and pay the yearly dues of $25. Clergy can be associate members but are not allowed to vote or hold office. The CBMC U.S.A. has about 10,000 members among businessmen and professionals in about 500 chapters throughout the United States. Local chapters generally meet weekly for lunch and listen to guest speakers, such as military men, police officers, attorneys, and prominent business leaders, tell about their Christian experience. The CBMC U.S.A. publishes a bimonthly magazine for its members, *Contact,* and holds a well-attended annual convention. In 1977 that convention met at the elegant Hotel Del Coronado, San Diego, California. Said Paul Johnson, former CBMC International chairman, about the hotel:

> It's quite a contrast to the concrete and glass of so many hotels. It's got the beautiful white, sandy beach, tennis courts, palm trees. The woodwork is fantastic. It's a real historic place . . . a charming, gracious touch of the old world. . . .
>
> The Hotel Del Coronado is a really first-class hotel . . . the type we should go to every year at convention time.[1]

Typical of CBMC U.S.A. special events was the Honor Police Officers Night, sponsored by CBMC of Greater Los Angeles at the Huntington Sheraton Hotel in 1976. The dinner featured Los Angeles police chief Ed Davis, a notable spokesman for law and order, and 240 lawmen as guests.[2]

Charismatics also have an organization of this nature, the Full Gospel Business Men's Fellowship International (Los Angeles), founded in 1951 by ex-dairyman Demos Shakarian. Like the CBMC U.S.A., the FGBMFI is made up of laymen in business and the professions in more than 700 chapters in the United States and Canada. It publishes a monthly magazine, *Voice,* and holds an annual convention (international in scope) at a luxury hotel in addition to the weekly breakfast, luncheon, or dinner meetings held by local chapters. But the FGBMFI differs from the CBMC U.S.A. in its de-emphasis of doctrine and its stress on religious experience (Spirit baptism), its larger number of minority members, and its high percentage of Roman Catholic members (characteristic of charismatic renewal as a whole). Although the ethos of the FGBMFI is indeed conservative, it is generally more open in its religious, cultural, and political concerns than the CBMC U.S.A. Popular speakers include not only prominent business leaders and military men but also leading charismatic (Protestant and Catholic) clergy and even academics.

WOMEN'S ORGANIZATIONS

Center and right evangelical women have a low-profile national fellowship and evangelistic organization, the Christian Women's Clubs, with national headquarters (Stonecroft Ministries) in Kansas City, Missouri. Local chapters are Christian counterparts to the traditional secular women's clubs. Oriented chiefly around the needs and interests of the typical suburban evangelical housewife, luncheon meetings of the Christian Women's Clubs feature fashion shows, cooking and makeup instruction, music by Christian entertainers, and addresses by a variety of speakers. Childcare is usually provided, and announcements of scheduled gatherings are often made over the local Christian radio stations. Stonecraft also has an organization for business and professional women.

An interesting recent development for right and center evangelical women has been the emergence of the Patricia French Christian Charm Schools and Patricia French Cosmetics. As seen in her ads and photos in leading evangelical magazines, French is a very attractive "actress and television personality" who is heard regularly on Christian radio in New York, Chicago, San Francisco, Los Angeles, and other major cities. The Patricia French Christian Charm Schools offer franchises to interested individuals—"a unique business opportunity for teaching Christian women of all ages who desire to improve their poise, voice, diction, personality, social graces, and appearance." Patricia French Cosmetics are created "especially for Christian women" who want to "look younger". Indeed, French has been advertising an "introductory beauty kit" for $39.95. Long gone are the days when evangelical women could be distinguished from their secular counterparts by their very moderate or total lack of makeup and their slightly out-of-style plain or businesslike dress (witness the repeal of dress codes over the last several years at leading evangelical colleges). In fact, many center and right evangelical women now try to be first with the latest in fashions and cosmetics.

THE FAMILY AND BILL GOTHARD'S INSTITUTES IN BASIC YOUTH CONFLICTS

The centrality of the nuclear family and the traditional roles of husband, wife, and children within that family are strongly affirmed by right and center evangelicals. In reaction to the fact that liberal Protestant leaders and the public more generally (not to mention the evangelical left) are questioning those domestic values, evangelicals of the center and right are reading and writing books supporting the traditional view (Larry Christenson's best-selling *The Christian Family* is a prime example), and are flocking by the thousands to Bill Gothard's Institutes in Basic Youth Conflicts, held in major population areas of the United States.

Gothard, a rather colorless and hardly scintillating 43-year-old graduate of Wheaton College and former Chicago area youth minister, developed his theories of dealing with the problems of youth and the family during the mid-60s while working in local churches, where his ideas met with considerable success. The word spread around, interest heightened, and, by the mid-70s, Bill Gothard could attract 28,000 people at a time to his 6-day, 32-hour institutes convened numerous times each year. Like Werner Erhard's "est" programs, Gothard's institutes are not advertised. Individuals hear about them by word of mouth alone. Students are even asked not to share their course notebooks and other materials with others.

The Institutes in Basic Youth Conflicts are made up entirely of lectures by Bill Gothard—no entertainment, no workshops, and no small-group work. Students pay a $50 registration fee, and graduates can take refresher courses free (former students are sent birthday cards, and their names are listed as potential prayer partners). Gothard has a growing staff to coordinate the institutes and is planning a school in Oak Brook, Illinois, to produce teachers of his concepts. He is unmarried, lives modestly with his parents (just as he encourages other unmarried to do), and puts much of the money he earns back into his ministry.

Bill Gothard's institutes are a blend largely of Scripture, taken literally, psychology and common sense, based upon traditional American Protestant values. For Gothard the Bible has the answer to all our problems (there is much proof-texting in the institutes). The instructor provides his students with numerous lists of biblical principles to deal with major and minor life issues, from education to vocation, from dating and petting to raising a family. Gothard's program for successful Christian living is centered on the nuclear family, governed by a strict chain of command, in which the husband, submitting to the rule of God over his life, is head of the home. The wife submits to his authority in toto (a "bad" decision of the husband is better than a "good" decision of the wife), and children obey their parents without question and submit to their will until marriage.

Widespread criticism of Gothard focuses on what the critics see as his unrealistic authoritarian models, his abdication of responsibility to others unjustifiably, his twisting of Scripture to fit preconceived theories, and his simplistic answers to complex life problems. Nevertheless, the crowds attending Bill Gothard's Institutes in Basic Youth Conflicts are not diminishing. Furthermore, the institutes are attended not only by evangelicals but also by Protestant liberals and Roman Catholics who are tired of their churches' and ministers' inability or refusal to provide concrete answers to their questions about life and how to live it. Gothard is good at giving straightforward answers unabashedly; and for the thousands and thousands of his faithful disciples, they have apparently rung true.[3]

The ideal right or center evangelical family is indeed committed to a traditional, culturally conservative lifestyle. Much, if not most, of the time, family members are involved in the church and its activities. Secular pastimes are still often frowned upon. But one totally acceptable activity for center and right evangelicals, as both spectators and participants, is sports. Evangelicals believe that sports are clean and healthy and build good character. The media are filled with reports of prominent athletes, players and coaches, amateurs and professionals, who became successful when they committed their lives to Christ. Oral Roberts University (known for its first-rate basketball team) emphasizes athletic prowess and physical fitness to the point that all students and faculty are required to participate in a physical fitness program (aerobics) and are strongly encouraged to support the school's teams, which are treated royally.

I have already mentioned Campus Crusade's Athletes in Action, a fellowship and evangelistic organization of evangelical athletes who are committed to aggressive evangelism. Another important, but far more subdued, low-profile, and theologically rather inclusive, organization of Christian sports enthusiasts is the Fellowship of Christian Athletes (FCA). With headquarters in Kansas City, FCA was founded in 1955 and has chapters in more than 1600 high schools and 250 colleges and universities in the United States. Almost all pro football teams have players and/or coaches affiliated with the FCA, and many prominent athletes are recruited to help out with special FCA programs and summer camps, all of which are well attended.[4]

The one interchurch activity that includes liberal congregations of which conservative evangelical churches almost universally approve is competitive team sports. Even the most conservative congregations are often willing to pit their crack softball or basketball teams against foes from local liberal Protestant or Roman Catholic churches. Just as in the wider society, sports, in the Christian context, somehow transcend ideological barriers.

SEX AND THE TOTAL WOMAN (AND MAN)

With the sexual revolution and the advance of the permissive society, center and right evangelicals have also "gotten in touch with their bodies"—in marriage, at least. In *The Young Evangelicals,* I suggested that evangelicals enjoy sex too, but are afraid to admit it. Today, they shout it from the house tops.

Marabel Morgan was recently the subject of a *Time* magazine cover story (March 14, 1977). Author of *The Total Woman,* and its sequel, *Total Joy,* Morgan is an ex-beauty queen and former Campus Crusade for Christ staffer. Like other right and center evangelicals, she, too, insists on the traditional wife-subordinate-to-her-husband marital role, almost to an extreme. In fact, the central message of *The Total Woman* is: "Please your husband!" By making *him* the center of her life (next to God, of course), a Christian wife can find total fulfillment. "I do believe it is possible," says Morgan, "for almost any wife to have her husband absolutely adore her in just a few weeks' time. She can revive romance, reestablish communication, break down barriers, and put sizzle back into her marriage. It really is up to her" (p. 20).

Morgan dwells at length on common-sense ways for a wife to please her husband, but her chief concern is teaching wives how to "turn on" their husbands sexually. Morgan feels that by pleasing her husband sexually, a wife can get almost anything from him. Morgan's philosophy of total womanhood is detailed in her Total Woman courses taught across the United States by her trained disciples.

In *The Total Woman,* published originally in 1973, the author devotes three chapters to sex in marriage. Her rather explicit advice shocked evangelical booksellers. At first, the book had to be special ordered; then it was kept under the counter in conservative Bible bookstores. Finally, however, *The Total Woman* became a bestseller among center and right evangelical women and others, because Morgan does keep sex in marriage. According to the Bible, the marriage bed is "undefiled," so let's take advantage of it. If evangelical wives and husbands had been sexually repressed before, Marabel Morgan was the catalyst that changed their unhappy situation. And that is the true significance of *The Total Woman.*

The book itself is full of quotable quotes: "Your husband loves your body; in fact, he literally craves it" (p. 112). "He wants the girl of his dreams to be feminine, soft, and touchable when he comes home" (p. 113). "Your husband needs you to fulfill his daydreams" (p. 117).

"Sex is an hour in bed at ten o'clock; super sex is the climax of an atmosphere that has been carefully set all day" (p. 144). "Eat by candlelight; you'll light his candle" (p. 148). "For a change tonight, after the children are in bed, place a lighted candle on the floor and seduce him under the dining-room table" (p. 153).

Since *The Total Woman*, a plethora of books dealing explicitly with sex and sensuousness in marriage have emerged from the pens of right and center evangelicals. Important among these are *The Total Man* by former Campus Crusade for Christ staffer Dan Benson; *Intended for Pleasure* by Ed Wheat and Gaye Wheat; and *A Song for Lovers* by S. Craig Glickman, a *literal* study of The Song of Solomon (hitherto evangelicals have taken the book as an allegory, neglecting its erotic frankness). But the groundbreaking work on marital sex technique for conservative evangelicals is Tim LaHaye and Beverly LaHaye's *The Act of Marriage*. A "more biblical" and less crude manual than Alex Comfort's *The Joy of Sex* (New York: Crown, 1972), which many evangelicals still read. *The Act of Marriage* was designated by *Christianity Today* (March 18, 1977) as one of the "25 choice evangelical books of 1976." In it, the LaHayes destroy the last vestiges of sexual repression in marriage.

Tim and Beverly LaHaye devote one chapter to the results of a sex survey they conducted among 1705 women and 1672 men (all married) who had attended their Family Life Seminars across the United States, 98 percent of whom professed to be born-again Christians. In this sample, many of the wives had been influenced by *The Total Woman*. Seventy-seven percent of them were experiencing orgasm regularly, 11 percent periodically. Sixty-eight percent of the wives and 67 percent of the husbands confessed that the men manipulated their wife's clitoris orally, while only 11 percent of the wives and 8 percent of the husbands admitted that the women helped their husbands achieve orgasm by oral stimulation of the penis regularly (15 percent periodically, however). More than 35 percent of the couples were having intercourse 3–6 times per week (average age: husbands, late 30s; wives, mid-30s). Seventy-three percent of the wives polled were regularly satisfied with intercourse, 19 percent periodically satisfied. And, most interesting of all, 81 percent of the wives and 85 percent of the husbands rated their love life as "above average and very happy" (pp. 195–217).

If we are to believe the LaHayes' survey—a recent *Redbook* poll discovered that "the strongly religious woman seems to be even more responsive [sexually] than other women her age"[5]—center and right evangelicals are no longer as frustrated sexually as they were made out to be. Marital fidelity in a permissive society, insisted upon by evangelicals, apparently has its own rewards.

The evangelical right and center is getting harder to distinguish from the wider society physically, socially, and politically. Right and center evangelicals are richer, better educated, better dressed, and better fed than they used to be. Furthermore, they are more materialistic than they were in the past. *Success* is a very important word in their vocabulary because, by the world's standards, they *have* become successful. Most important of all, these evangelicals are now respectable.

Theologically, center and right evangelicals stand squarely in the tradition of the Protestant work ethic. More of them are joining and becoming active in churches of the historic mainline denominations. With their increasing numerical strength, they are making their presence in these churches felt by the liberal denominational leadership. Television and radio, Christian men's and women's clubs have replaced the revival tent and tracts as the locus of their evangelism. Theology is still important to right and center evangelicals; they continue unashamedly to defend the authority of the Bible, the need for conversion, and the mandate for evangelism. But their religious style has become more subdued, more middle-class.

In response to pressure from the evangelical left, the media, and the wider society as a whole, center and right evangelicals have become more sensitized to current social issues but still move cautiously in working for social change, especially when it involves a challenge to their comfortable economic status, which represents God's blessing on them and their families.

How are right and center evangelicals different from the wider culture? Almost all of them seem to have discovered a good measure of direction, meaning, purpose, and vocation in their personal lives—qualities lacking in much of the wider society. Witness their smiling faces on television and local billboards. This is where Jesus fits in. Indeed, the basic stance of center and right evangelicals is summarized well by the slogan "I found it!" They have, or at least they *think* they have.

These evangelicals feel that by their presence and witness they are transforming the wider secular society and its values. But it might be much more accurate to suggest that the wider culture is transforming *them*. And the question that faces all Christians remains unanswered— what will we do with the cross? Wear it, or bear it?

Part III

THE YOUNG
EVANGELICAL LEFT

7

Theological Convictions

By and large, twentieth-century white evangelicals have either been outwardly apolitical or have taken the conservative position on almost every social, economic, and political issue. For a long time there has been a visible alliance between the evangelical right and center and the Republican Party, culminating perhaps in the Billy Graham–Richard Nixon friendship and the evangelist's public endorsement of Nixon's presidential candidacy in 1972.

Evangelicals did not so uniformly identify themselves with the status quo in the past. Nineteenth-century leaders—especially those grounded in the Wesleyan, holiness, or New School Presbyterian traditions (which, unlike the Old School, favored revivalism), such as Jonathan Blanchard (founder of Wheaton College in Illinois), revivalist Charles G. Finney, Phoebe Palmer (Methodist lay evangelist), and William Booth and Catherine Booth (co-founders of The Salvation Army)—were influential in the abolitionist and feminist struggles of their day.[1]

At the triennial missionary convention of Inter-Varsity Christian Fellowship (IVCF), Urbana '70, it became clear that a new generation of young evangelicals (as I have termed them) who repudiate the modern alliance of theological conservatism with political, social, and cultural conservatism in America was emerging. The college, university, and seminary students in attendance and their invited speakers surprised the evangelical establishment by denouncing what they viewed as the blatantly racist character of white evangelical churches and United States participation in the Vietnam War.

From that major beginning, the discontent among young evangelicals (and their older sympathizers) became increasingly visible until about 50 of them, together with a few evangelical elder statesmen like Carl F. H. Henry, Rufus Jones of the Conservative Baptist Home Mission Society, and Frank E. Gaebelein, headmaster emeritus of The Stony Brook School in New York, hammered out the much publicized Chicago Declaration of Evangelical Social Concern over the Thanksgiving weekend in 1973. This statement is a confession of evangelical complicity in the racism, sexism, militarism, and economic injustice of the wider U. S. society.[2] Even *Newsweek* (May 6, 1974, p. 86) called attention to the leftward trend of contemporary evangelicalism, while *National Review* (February 15, 1974, pp. 192–194) lamented the fact that evangelicals could no longer be counted on to support en masse the conservative Republican stance.

As I said earlier, the vanguard of the evangelical left is centered on a small, highly literate, zealous, and generally younger elite, many of whose spokespersons helped formulate the Chicago Declaration. Evangelicals of the left range from moderate Republicans to democratic socialists, if not Marxists. Most affirm the nuclear family but are at the same time open to alternative domestic lifestyles, from extended families to communes. Just about all of the left evangelicals are feminists and support the ordination of women, egalitarian marriage, and the use of inclusive language. The old evangelical taboos against alcohol, tobacco, social dancing, and the like are almost universally condemned (as binding, at least). Biblical criticism, used constructively and devoutly, is employed by a great many evangelical students and scholars of the left. They recognize the marks of cultural conditioning on Scripture, and their study of the Bible is informed by their knowledge of the natural, social, and behavioral sciences. Within the evangelical community as a whole, evangelicals of the left are probably a small minority at the present time, but an increasingly vocal and influential one, to say the least.

Fuller Seminary and "Limited Inerrancy"

Without a doubt, Fuller Theological Seminary is the foremost center of theological education and scholarship in the evangelical world. It is also the leading center of learning for the evangelical left. In this regard, we can point to the progressive, if not avant-garde, works of the venerable George E. Ladd in New Testament theology and exegesis; Paul K. Jewett in systematic theology; James Daane in theology and ministry; Ralph Martin in New Testament; Lewis B. Smedes in theology and ethics; Daniel P. Fuller in hermeneutics (principles of biblical interpretation); Jack Rogers in theology and philosophy of religion; Bill Pannell in evangelism and black ministries; Ray S. Anderson in systematic theology; Joy Wilt in Christian education; Charles H. Kraft in missionary anthropology and African studies; and H. Newton Malony and Neil Clark Warren in psychology.

Fuller Seminary was founded in 1947 and has expanded into three graduate schools occupying eight acres in Pasadena, California, and six extension centers in various parts of the United States. In addition to the original School of Theology, there is also a School of World Mission (established in 1965) and a School of Psychology (also begun in 1965), which awards the Ph.D. in clinical psychology and is accredited by the American Psychological Association (the only seminary school of its kind so accredited). As of November 1976 Fuller boasted a full-time faculty of 46 and 61 part-time instructors, 1553 students on the Pasadena campus from almost every state and 30 foreign countries, with graduates of nearly 200 colleges and universities (making it the largest nondenominational seminary in the country). Students represented over 80 denominations, the largest contingent from The United Presbyterian Church in the U.S.A. (a group so large that it is threatening even to the best United Presbyterian seminaries).

All of Fuller's regular degree curricula are among the most rigorous and demanding of their kind in the United States (witness the impressive record of Fuller students on the standardized United Presbyterian preordination examinations). Many graduates of the seminary have gone on to the most prestigious universities in the world for doctoral work and are already making their mark on religious scholarship. Fuller has one of the best placement records in the country, and its M.Div. graduates have distinguished themselves as pastors and youth ministers both in the historic mainline denominations and in those we have termed distinctively evangelical.

Like other seminaries in the United States, Fuller has greatly increased

the number of women and minority students in all its programs, the
M.Div. in particular. It has established special curricula in black and
Hispanic ministries. Students come to Fuller Seminary from a wide variety of theological and ecclesiastical traditions (including the Roman
Catholic Church), and there is much freedom of thought and lifestyle on
the campus. Chapel services are attended by students and faculty on a
voluntary basis, and there is no dress or behavior code imposed. Under
the influence of Professor Robert Boyd Munger, "relational theology"
has become an important part of student life over the last several years.
Immediately upon their arrival, new students are placed in a support
group of other students to help them grow spiritually, improve their
interpersonal relationships, and integrate their classwork with their intended vocation. Many of the seminary's graduates take this small-group
experience with them as a model for their own parish ministries. I believe
that Fuller Theological Seminary is now the best Protestant seminary in
the United States (if not the world) for the training of pastors, youth
ministers, missionaries, and clinical psychologists.

Much of Fuller's recent success can be credited directly to the leadership of David Hubbard, the seminary's president. In fact, of all contemporary evangelical leaders, he is the person to watch. An Old Testament
scholar, Hubbard was inaugurated as president in 1963, when he was
only 36, and Fuller Seminary had just 300 students. President Hubbard
has since that time proved himself to be an ecclesiastical statesman par
excellence and a very smooth administrator. He is an ordained American
Baptist minister and impresses everyone with his preaching ability,
charm, and political savvy. Hubbard was a theological adviser to the
Fifth General Assembly of the World Council of Churches (Nairobi,
1975) and co-chairperson of The Danforth Foundation and Lilly Endowment's recent national and regional consultations on "dialogue with
evangelicals in campus ministry." At present he serves on the board of
directors of the National Institute for Campus Ministries (Protestant, Catholic, and Jewish) and is completing a two-year term as president of the
Association of Theological Schools (ATS) in the United States and Canada, the accreditation body for all North American theological seminaries.
Hubbard was for three years a member of the California State Board of
Education, and, in the course of that term of service, he voted *against* requiring public schools in the state to teach "creation" rather than evolu-

tion. As better relationships between evangelicals and Protestant liberals (and Roman Catholics) continue to develop, David Hubbard is bound to be an increasingly prominent contributor to the process.

We have already noted that Fuller Seminary has been surrounded by controversy since its founding. In 1976 Harold Lindsell published his famous, or infamous, book, *The Battle for the Bible*. In it the author documents for the reading public what insiders have known all along, that the doctrine of total inerrancy is no longer taught at Fuller, and that its importance in the Southern Baptist Convention, The Lutheran Church–Missouri Synod, and elsewhere in the evangelical world is declining rapidly. This public exposé is highly significant, because what happened originally at Fuller Seminary in the mid-60s is now an increasingly dominant trend in almost all prominent (and some not so prominent) evangelical seminaries and colleges in the United States, whether their board members and administrative officers admit it or not, and whether their statement of faith contains a total inerrancy clause or not.

The roots of the inerrancy doctrine can be traced to the seventeenth-century Westminster Confession of Faith (though the Reformers themselves never really questioned the complete veracity of Scripture) and, more directly, to the Reformed scholasticism of Charles Hodge and Archibald Alexander Hodge, Benjamin B. Warfield, and the Old Princeton school of theology they represented in the late nineteenth and early twentieth centuries. Gradually, in the course of the fundamentalist–modernist dispute and its aftermath, even pietist, Wesleyan, holiness, and pentecostal groups that once had been far more concerned about right conduct and spirituality than about correct doctrine per se moved toward the total inerrancy position that stressed an intellectual assent to doctrinal propositions *over* the holy living, with its personal and social aspects, emphasized by their forebears.

With the inroads of modern science and biblical criticism into American evangelical circles, however, the total inerrancy position has become increasingly difficult to maintain; it never took root among the leading evangelicals in Great Britain and the Continent. Thus a doctrine of *limited inerrancy* began to be promulgated at Fuller Seminary during the 60s, championed by Charles Fuller's son, Daniel, who was then dean of the School of Theology, and was finally, in 1972, incorporated into the seminary's statement of faith. The original clause declared the Bible to be "free from all error in the whole and in the part." The new wording says: "All the books of the Old and New Testaments, given by divine inspiration, are the written word of God, the only infallible rule of faith and practice."

The position affirming that Scripture is inerrant or infallible in its teaching on matters of faith and conduct, but not necessarily in all its assertions concerning history and the cosmos, is gradually becoming ascendant among the most highly respected evangelical theologians. They feel strongly that the doctrine of limited inerrancy both preserves the Bible's authority for the church and makes feasible the use of the literary-historical-critical method in studying its contents.

As profound as the shift from total to limited inerrancy has been for the evangelicals, more recent developments indicate further changes in the evangelical left's attitude toward the inspiration and authority of Scripture. A bombshell hit the evangelical community in 1975 when Paul K. Jewett published his positive theological treatment of feminism, *Man as Male and Female,* which he had circulated among his students at Fuller for years prior to its publication. Jewett emphasized the cultural conditioning of the Bible more than any previous evangelical theologian had done. He challenged the limited inerrancy position (indirectly, at least) by stating that Paul, in his teaching about the subordination of women to men, was influenced both by his male-dominated culture and by rabbinic traditions representing a time-bound authority not applicable to later Christians in other cultures. In a word, Paul was *wrong.*

Understandably, Jewett's new hermeneutic has rocked the conservative evangelical establishment (it was the last straw for Lindsell). Those affirming limited inerrancy, though somewhat disturbed, seem less shaken. What is most interesting, however, is the fact that a large number of younger evangelicals scoff altogether at their elders' stress on inerrancy by whatever definition. They insist that a precise doctrine of the inspiration and authority of Scripture is far less important than unconditional obedience to what it demands, arguing that those Christians most committed to inerrancy have tended to be the least passionate about the biblical requirements of social justice, righteousness, and peace. All this suggests a growing shift among evangelicals of the left from viewing the Bible as the divine revelation of propositional truth and doctrine to understanding it *functionally*, seeing the significance of Scripture in the way it transforms people individually and collectively. In other words, revelation comes as a *result* of obedience, not vice versa.

The crux of Lindsell's argument with Fuller Seminary is that once a seminary begins to challenge inerrancy it will eventually end up in the liberal camp entirely. He cites the history of the mainline denominational and ecumenical schools of theology that were founded as orthodox institutions of theological learning but, in the course of their development, gradually moved all the way toward the theological left. Lindsell is correct. The catalyst of this shift *was* the seminaries' questioning of the absolute authority of the Bible. Yet in almost every case, the first biblical critics at these seminaries were faithful church people, devout and committed, who felt that what they were saying and doing about Scripture was merely an expression of their intellectual honesty and their faithfulness to the Gospel. Such has been the reaction of David Hubbard and Fuller Seminary as a whole to Lindsell's charges which, except in a few factual details, they have not been able to refute. (Lindsell could have also mentioned the strong secularizing trend in the School of Psychology and the radical anthropological studies being conducted in the School of World Mission.)

Both sides of the controversy feel that God is on their side. But it is Fuller Seminary rather than Lindsell that stands to lose most if it loses the battle. The seminary relies on gifts and grants to provide about 25 percent of its annual budget. Much of this money has traditionally come from theological conservatives who were troubled to learn the details of Lindsell's account.

To counter the effect of *The Battle for the Bible,* Hubbard gave a powerful and moving convocation address in April 1976, prior to the book's publication, affirming in no uncertain terms Fuller Seminary's commitment to the authority of the Bible as the word of God written. Later he articulated Fuller's position further in a widely distributed booklet, "What We Believe and Teach." These efforts were followed by a costly public relations campaign that included a series of full-page ads in the leading evangelical magazines focusing on some of the seminary's most prominent graduates and their appreciation of Fuller's biblical teaching and commitment. A special issue of *Theology, News and Notes,* the Seminary's alumni/ae journal, was published in 1976 to answer Lindsell's charges. Old Testament Professor William S. LaSor presented his own version of Fuller's stormy history, contradicting Lindsell at a few points but not really denying the thrust of the latter's argument. (Other articles in that issue serve more to clarify and defend the seminary's current position than to accuse the critical conservative evangelical author of blatant falsehood.) All of these concerns prompted a book to be written as an evangelical alternative to *The Battle for the Bible* and its insistance that total inerrancy is the evangelical watershed. Edited by Jack Rogers, the work is entitled *Biblical Authority*, and contains essays by several leading evangelicals of the left including Hubbard, Clark Pinnock, Bernard Ramm, Earl Palmer, and Rogers himself. The battle at Fuller Seminary is not ended yet, but it is clear that Lindsell's book has not been as devastating as originally supposed; 85 percent of its graduates would choose Fuller again. [3]

Other Seminaries

Slightly to the left of Fuller Seminary stands Seminex (Concordia Seminary in Exile) in St. Louis, another increasingly visible graduate school of theology representing the evangelical left. Seminex is a theological seminary in the "confessing" movement (the moderates) that has emerged from within The Lutheran Church–Missouri Synod. It has an interdependent relationship with that movement, expressed originally in an organization within the Missouri Synod, Evangelical Lutherans in Mission (ELIM), and now in an emerging denomination still in formation, the Association of Evangelical Lutheran Churches (AELC). Seminex is an independently incorporated seminary with its own governing board, sharing the facilities of St. Louis University and Eden Theological Seminary (United Church of Christ), Webster Groves, Missouri, and serving interested Lutheran congregations and agencies, primarily within the Missouri Synod and the AELC. Headed by John H. Tietjen, Seminex declares that "the Sacred Scriptures of the Old and the New Testaments are the only rule and norm of faith and practice and . . . the Lutheran Symbols [confessions] are a true and faithful statement and exposition of the Word of God." [4]

Other prominent graduate schools of theology identified increasingly with the evangelical left include North Park Theological Seminary, Chicago; Bethel Theological Seminary, St. Paul; Gordon-Conwell Theological Seminary, South Hamilton, Massachusetts; Conservative Baptist Theological Seminary, Denver; Asbury Theological Seminary,

Wilmore, Kentucky; and the new charismatic School of Theology at Oral Roberts University, Tulsa.

North Park is controlled by the Evangelical Covenant Church of America, the most ecumenical distinctively evangelical denomination in the United States. Its catalogue affirms "the Holy Scriptures, the Old and the New Testament, as the Word of God and the only perfect rule for faith, doctrine, and conduct." Notable scholars of the evangelical left at the seminary include F. Burton Nelson in theology and ethics (editor of *The Covenant Quarterly*); and Donald W. Dayton, director of the Mellander Library.

Bethel is the theological seminary of the Baptist General Conference, but it stands far to the left of most Conference Baptist churches. Prominent left evangelical professors at Bethel include Clarence B. Bass, author of *Backgrounds to Dispensationalism,* an early refutation of dispensationalism that brought him much criticism from conservatives in the denomination; Robert Guelich, an up-and-coming critical New Testament scholar; A. Berkeley Mickelsen, another professor of New Testament and a contributor to Jack Rogers' *Biblical Authority;* and Garth M. Rosell, a church historian and son of the revivalist Merv Rosell. Bethel adheres formally to the statement of faith of the Baptist General Conference, which speaks of the Bible as "the Word of God, fully inspired and without error in the original manuscripts."

Gordon-Conwell, headed in recent years by Harold Ockenga, a staunch conservative who coined the term *neo-evangelical,* was once itself a bastion of political and theological conservatism. It is a nondenominational school that affirms that "The sixty-six canonical books of the Bible as originally written were inspired of God, hence free from error."[5] Notable scholars of the evangelical left at the seminary include Gordon D. Fee in New Testament; black historian of Christian thought Wesley A. Roberts; Stephen C. Mott in Christianity and urban society; Eldin Villafane in Christianity and society; Dean Borgman (a regional director of Young Life Campaign) in youth ministry; and Deane A. Kemper in applied ministry.

Conservative Baptist Theological Seminary in Denver is the "liberal" counterpart to strongly dispensational Western Conservative Baptist Theological Seminary in Portland, Oregon. One wonders how much longer the former seminary, headed by Vernon Grounds, a political liberal who recently resigned as secretary of the Evangelical Theological

Society, will be able to function successfully within the Conservative Baptist Association. Because of his politics and general openness in theology, Grounds is regularly accused of heresy by denominational conservatives (a genuinely ridiculous charge), and constantly finds himself in a political "hot seat" within the denomination. The faculty of Conservative Baptist Seminary are actually quite a bit more conservative than their counterparts at Bethel and Gordon-Conwell, but a few younger scholars at the seminary bear watching, including Robert L. Hubbard, Jr. (David Hubbard's nephew) in Old Testament, and Timothy P. Weber in church history.

Asbury, unlike the aforementioned schools, is a distinctively Wesleyan, Arminian theological seminary—nondenominational in character, but serving Methodists predominantly (in 1976, 352 out of 562 students were members of The United Methodist Church[6]). The seminary is committed to "the divine inspiration and infallibility of the Holy Scriptures," and all faculty must be "in full sympathy with the Wesleyan interpretation of the Scriptures on Entire Sanctification."[7] Gilbert M. James, professor of the church in society at Asbury, has been responsible for motivating many evangelical college students and seminarians to become interested in urban, inner-city ministries.

At this point a word should be said about the new School of Theology at Oral Roberts University in Tulsa, opened in 1976. This school, strangely enough, does not have a statement of faith, though all faculty members must conform to the university's "charismatic lifestyle", which resembles a kind of old-fashioned, nondoctrinal Methodist pietism adapted to the charismatic experience of Spirit baptism and the upwardly mobile atmosphere of Oral Roberts University (an "adult Disneyland," as someone has suggested). Roberts himself is a United Methodist minister and downplays the need for a rigid doctrinal stance. One can already sense among the School of Theology's faculty a strong interest in existentialism (reflective of Roberts' theology of "the now") and even the thought of Paul Tillich. But we shall have to wait and see before making a more definitive judgment.

Evangelical Liberal Arts Colleges

Liberal arts colleges related to the evangelical movement are generally to the left of its graduate schools of theology. Their governing boards usually do not watch them as closely, and their faculty members are most often not as visible as their seminary counterparts. Trinity College is more liberal than Trinity Evangelical Divinity School; Gordon College, more so than Gordon-Conwell Theological Seminary; Bethel and North Park Colleges, more so than Bethel Seminary and North Park Seminary. As Donald W. Dayton puts it, ''Some NAE colleges are to the left of Fuller Seminary in their use of critical methodologies [in the study of Scripture]. . . .''[8] The governing boards of these colleges are not blind to this situation. They know that many of their faculty sign the required statement of faith tongue in cheek. The same attitude pertains to faculty and students who break the conduct code (or pledge) imposed by some colleges banning gambling, alcohol, tobacco, pot, and social dancing on *and* off campus. In 1974, rumor had it that 70 percent of Wheaton College seniors were breaking the pledge, and there were stories of faculty and students meeting each other at nearby liquor stores. (Wheaton's prominent eastern and western counterparts—Gordon College, Wenham, Massachusetts; and Westmont College, Santa Barbara, California—have revoked their own pledges.) What *does* concern the governing boards of these colleges, however, is that the infringement of doctrinal standards and rules of conduct remain a local, ''in-house'' matter. As long as professors do not publish their liberal views in widely circulated popular magazines read by conservative financial backers of these institutions, much can be tolerated.

Of all the distinctively evangelical liberal arts colleges, Wheaton is the best and most important. The college that graduated Billy Graham, Carl F. H. Henry, and Harold Lindsell, to name a few, has been, in many ways, the hub of the evangelical establishment. But its Division of Biblical Studies is moving farther to the left, both in its utilization of critical methods and in the cultural attitudes and politics of its faculty. Most notable among Wheaton scholars in theology is Robert Webber, who is probably the college's most popular teacher. Early in his career at Wheaton, Webber was one of the persons responsible for replacing the then required freshman course in apologetics (defense of the faith) with a course in Christ and culture, in recognition of the crucial role of culture in a student's spiritual formation. Webber is unpopular, however, with a few of Wheaton's trustees. The reason for this disfavor has to do with Webber's political liberalism (he was a member of the Evangelicals for McGovern committee) together with his sacramental, Anglo-Catholic theology. His leadership in the organization of The Chicago Call, and the fact that he is an Episcopal layman illustrates the broadening out of evangelicalism at its center.

Like many other evangelical seminaries and colleges, Wheaton affirms the Bible as "verbally inspired by God and inerrant in the original writing." As a result of a recent creation–evolution dispute at the college, it added a clause on the matter to its statement of faith declaring that "Wheaton College is committed to the Biblical teaching that man was created by a direct act of God and not from previously existing forms of life; and that all men are descended from the historical Adam and Eve, first parents of the entire human race."[9] But. . . .

Concluding the discussion of centers of theological education and scholarship representing the evangelical left, I must mention Regent College, Vancouver, British Columbia, a unique graduate school of theology for the training of evangelical laity. Regent offers a two-year Master of Christian Studies degree, but it is much better known for its summer sessions, with courses taught by some of the most eminent evangelical scholars in the world. Headed by James M. Houston, formerly bursar of Oxford University's Hertford College, Regent was founded in 1968 by surprisingly open Plymouth Brethren. But the college is careful not to alienate its conservative financial contributors by hiring faculty who are deemed too liberal, in the public eye, at least. Most prominent among Regent's faculty are Carl E. Armerding in Old Testament, and W. Ward Gasque in New Testament.

Evangelical Scholars at Liberal Seminaries

Since the fundamentalist–modernist controversy, only a handful of distinctively evangelical scholars have been faculty members of liberal Protestant denominational and ecumenical seminaries. Even fewer have been professors in departments of religious studies at secular universities and liberal arts colleges. And most of these have had to take on an extremely low profile to be acceptable with their colleagues. Notable among them are Bruce Metzger in New Testament at Princeton Theological Seminary (he chairs the revision committee of the National Council of Churches' Revised Standard Version of the Bible); and Donald Bloesch in theology at Dubuque Theological Seminary (he is the author of numerous books on church renewal, and a theologian whose position is moving ever closer to that of Karl Barth). With the increasing intellectual sophistication of younger evangelical scholars, blacks and women among them, however, we shall probably see a good number of these academics finding teaching and research positions at even the best nonevangelical religious and secular institutions of higher learning. A few are already becoming visible, including Nancy Hardesty at Emory University's Candler School of Theology in Atlanta (in church history and women's studies); James Forbes at Union Theological Seminary in New York, a black pentecostal (in preaching); and Gerald Sheppard, an ordained Assemblies of God minister, also at Union (in Old Testament). Sheppard, moreover, may be the first white pentecostal to have become a regular faculty member of a liberal Protestant seminary in the United States.

The Theological Students Fellowship

To promote the evangelical witness on secular college and university campuses and at liberal Protestant denominational and ecumenical seminaries in North America, The Theological Students Fellowshilp (TSF) was recently organized as a less conservative alternative to the Evangelical Theological Society. TSF is related to Inter-Varsity Christian Fellowship and to the International Fellowship of Evangelical Students (IFES). With headquarters in London, IFES was founded in 1947 as "a free association in Christian fellowship of national evangelical student movements," such as IVCF in the United States. It now has at least 34 member movements in North and Latin America, Australia, Europe, Africa, and Asia. TSF "encourages students to work towards academic excellence within their schools and to advance an approach to the Bible that seeks to be both intellectually sound and grounded in a commitment to its authority and relevance."

With Clark Pinnock as coordinator, and Mark Branson as secretary (both are very ecumenical evangelicals of the left), TSF provides its members with a sophisticated theological journal, *Themelios*, published three times a year; an occasional newsletter providing excellent information on current theological trends; and notices of regional theological conferences sponsored by the organization. Membership in TSF, whose headquarters are in Madison, Wisconsin, is by agreement with its doctrinal basis, including "the unique Divine inspiration, entire trustworthiness and authority of the Bible." The organization *does* invite as "subscribers" interested students and graduates who are not prepared to affirm the TSF doctrinal basis. They, too, receive all the mailings and may attend the regional conferences. In this connection, Mark Branson has been traveling the country facilitating the establishment of Bible- and theological-study groups of evangelical and what he calls "moderate" scholars and students—a groundbreaking ecumenical effort by evangelicals in the United States at the level of serious theological dialogue.

RELATIONAL THEOLOGY

Relational theology emerged in the late 60s as a reaction against the rational and scholastic doctrinal emphases of many evangelical churches that totally neglected the relational aspect of the Gospel—the command to love God, and love one's neighbor. Traditionally, evangelicals have used the word *fellowship* to describe the relational quality of the Gospel. But in most evangelical churches, fellowship has been reserved for born-again believers alone, and even then it has often meant little more than "punch and cookies." Furthermore, that fellowship was rarely extended to vocal dissenters from the congregation's stance—those who by conviction or personality didn't fit in.

Most prominent among relational theologians are Keith Miller, an Episcopal layman, and author of many widely read books; Lloyd Ogilvie, senior minister of the First Presbyterian Church of Hollywood, California (who is also a charismatic); Lyman Coleman, author of the well-known *Serendipity* books for church young people and their leaders; and Bruce Larson, an ordained United Presbyterian minister and the movement's chief theoretician.

In *The Relational Revolution,* Larson insists that "the Kingdom of God is in truth the kingdom of right relationships"—to God, to one's self, to significant others (family, friends, and colleagues), and to the world (the rest of humanity "whom one can choose to love or ignore"). Relational theology has been profoundly influenced by the secular human potential movement and its psychological, relational, and small-group techniques and theories. Larson stresses his conviction that "the quality and scope of relationships and the ability and willingness to relate are marks of orthodoxy rather than doctrine, ethical performance or spiritual heroism." Theology is relational, not conceptual.

Although relational theology is biblical to the core (some, of course, would disagree), it avoids the use of traditional evangelical language, loaded with "cultural baggage," that offends nonevangelical participants. Many evangelicals look at relational theology as hopelessly liberal; and an equal number of liberals view it as crassly conservative. But this Christian expression of the human potential movement is really a kind of bridge-building enterprise between liberals who have denied the need for conversion to Christ and evangelicals who, in the past anyway, have rejected the mandate for social action. Thus Larson terms it a movement for "a new breed of people . . . discovering a position which is unashamedly conservative in theology and liberal in its view of man."

Resources for the movement include the Faith at Work organization (Columbia, Maryland); its monthly magazine *Faith at Work* (Waco, Texas); and its faith renewal teams, conferences, leadership training institutes, and seminary ministries to train future ministers in relational theology. Also important are the books written by Larson, Coleman, Ogilvie, and Miller, and their periodic gatherings held across the United States in major convention centers and hotels, where participants are urged to "let it all hang out." In addition, Word, Inc. is publishing what will surely be a highly controversial relational theology church school curriculum designed by Joy Wilt of Fuller Seminary.

In *Ask Me to Dance,* Bruce Larson summarizes the themes of his work—"The Jesus Style in Relationships"—which shock many center and right evangelicals: (1) Be real. (Don't try to be like any other Christian or even like Jesus. Don't try to be spiritual.) (2) Identify with people. (3) Listen to people. (4) Affirm people. (5) Share decision making. (6) Don't try to change people. (To press for change, however subtly, indicates that the person is unacceptable as he is.) (7) Love specifically. (Love one person at a time and love that person in specific ways.) (8) Ask for help. (9) Love in terms meaningful to the other person. (10) Don't "play it safe." (There is risk in loving . . . the risk of being laughed at, misunderstood, and rejected.)[10] These are hard words for traditional evangelicals who, in their own Christian commitment and vocation, feel that they must love everyone (but in reality often love no one), are too busy with "the Lord's work" to be a close friend to anyone (even their own spouse), and too often "lay their evangelical trip" on people without regard for who they are and "where they're at."

THE CHARISMATIC RENEWAL MOVEMENT

More important, however, than relational theology in its effect on the evangelical left has been the charismatic renewal movement. Despite the materialism (brought about by upward social mobility) and near-fundamentalism of many charismatics, the movement as a whole has introduced a grassroots kind of ecumenism to evangelicals that they had never known before and thought was impossible without close doctrinal agreement. Because of the emphasis on religious experience in Spirit baptism, and the relative openness on lifestyle issues, Christians from the right to the left (including conservative evangelicals and Protestant liberals, too) have been united in fellowship, worship, and prayer in charismatic churches and informal gatherings. Religious liberals (Unitarian–Universalists, for instance) have a much easier time focusing on the experience of the Holy Spirit than on the orthodox doctrines of Christ. Likewise, even political, social, and cultural radicals can find some charismatic groups where they are welcome (especially in Roman Catholic circles). Although there was considerable friction at first between the pentecostal right and the Catholic charismatic left over doctrinal and lifestyle concerns, participants of both sides have found that their differences are minor compared to their unity in the experience of Spirit baptism.[11]

In summary, then, we can say that, although the evangelical left has no uniform theological stance, it does display certain dominant trends. The evangelical left stresses the functional power of the Bible to transform individuals and their social structures over the traditional evangelical understanding of Scripture as the depository of divine revelation and propositional truth in words alone. Left evangelicals, in their intellectual sophistication, study the Bible utilizing all forms of biblical criticism (devoutly), broad cultural analysis, and the results of social-scientific scholarship. There is among them a strong (but still emerging) emphasis on ecumenism, the existential *experience* of God, and on the relational character of theology. Conversion is still necessary, but it is now largely a matter of the transformation of one's life in the here and now rather than a matter for the hereafter. Biblical literalism is rejected to the point that evolution, no less than feminism, can be harmonized with the Scriptures. The Bible may indeed be the word of God, but it is also the word of human writers, and it bears the marks of cultural conditioning. Thus older concepts of inerrancy and infallibility are being interpreted in such a way as to focus on the biblical message of salvation rather than on the text itself. For many evangelicals of the left, the appropriate word to describe the Bible is *authoritative*, not infallible or inerrant.

In recent years left evangelical scholars have tried hard not to pit the word of God written against the dynamic, revealed Word of God, Jesus Christ himself, who is encountered through the action of the Holy Spirit on an individual, often in the context of the Christian community of faith (a stance characteristic of neo-orthodoxy). But the paradox here may now be too difficult for these evangelicals to accept, for they are moving ever closer to a position, like Barth's, where the Word is mediated in and through the reading of Scripture, which is the definitive *witness* to divine revelation (more than, or rather than, revelation itself). We encounter Christ and are transformed by him in reading and obeying the Bible. Hence, an inerrant biblical text loses its crucial importance. So what if there are a few "mistakes" in Scripture. The Bible is authoritative, but only indirectly. It gets its authority from Jesus Christ, to whom it bears witness. Earl Palmer, senior minister of the First Presbyterian Church of Berkeley, California, puts it well in his contribution to Jack Rogers' *Biblical Authority:*

> All doctrine must be tested by its submission to the historical witness that surrounds Jesus Christ, namely, the Bible, consisting of the Old Testament and the New Testament. As we trust in Jesus Christ, we trust in the witness to him. We have been convinced by the Holy Spirit of the Jesus Christ we met in the biblical witness to him (p. 131).

For evangelicals neo-orthodoxy has been a loaded term with many negative connotations. In reality it was merely an attempt, signaled initially by the publication in German of Barth's commentary on *The Epistle to the Romans* (1919), to repudiate—in the context of the crisis of World War I—liberalism's overly positive assessment of the human condition, its one-sided emphasis on the immanence of God in the world, and its view of the Bible as merely the record of the religious experiences of Israel. To counter liberal theology (the weaknesses of which were made even clearer with the advent of World War II), neo-orthodox theologians stressed the Reformation doctrine of the inherent sinfulness of humanity, the transcendance of God above his creation (his otherness), and Scripture as the sufficient and definitive witness to Christ who is the supreme authority for the church (rather than the Bible per se).

In *The Young Evangelicals,* I suggested that neo-orthodoxy had died with the emergence in the 60s of a new radical liberalism or secular Christianity. I argued that neo-orthodoxy, with its emphasis on Christ rather than the Bible itself as the final authority for the church, functioned as a far too nebulous system of thought—too difficult for ordinary laity, at least, to understand and apply to the concrete faith and conduct issues of life. But I was wrong. Indeed, the new theological heroes of the evangelical left are Karl Barth, Emil Brunner, and Dietrich Bonhoeffer, while they were living the foremost spokespersons of neo-orthodoxy on the Continent. Reinhold Niebuhr, its most articulate American representative, has also become popular among many left evangelicals. The works of these theologians are studied and taught sympathetically in evangelical seminaries. Evangelical scholars are writing an ever increasing number of articles and books paying high tribute to them. And the Karl Barth Society has so many applications for membership from evangelicals that it doesn't know what to do with them. (Strange goings on for leaders of a movement that ten years ago considered neo-orthodoxy and its theologians almost as dangerous as liberalism.) Clearly and undisputedly, the evangelical left is far closer to Bonhoeffer, Brunner, and Barth than to the Hodges and Warfield on the inspiration and authority of Scripture. And it may not be surprising if, despite David Hubbard's words to the contrary, Fuller Seminary eventually becomes the leading center of neo-orthodox conviction in the world—both in theology and in the critical study of Scripture.[12] In fact, the early demise of neo-orthodoxy in ecumenical circles may have been due to the fact that it had been born in liberalism. Neo-orthodoxy, carried and nurtured by evangelical theology, may prove to be stronger and more durable.

8

Evangelical Outreach

It is probably not an exaggeration to say that the campus and youth ministries (parachurch organizations, as they are called) of the evangelical left are among the most creative and effective of their kind anywhere. Like Campus Crusade for Christ, most of them were born in the cultural ethos of modern revivalism. But, unlike Crusade, they have changed dramatically in recent years and are now very much in step with the theological and cultural trends of the evangelical left as a whole. In fact, all these ministries see themselves as a more liberal alternative to Crusade's efforts at the college, university, and high school level in the United States and abroad. The youth and campus ministries of the evangelical left take on a quiet and intellectually sophisticated low profile, shunning publicity and the Madison Avenue techniques employed by Campus Crusade. Yet many nonevangelical clergy and laity still harbor an outdated stereotype of these organizations that no longer pertains.

Inter-Varsity Christian Fellowship

Inter-Varsity Christian Fellowship (IVCF) is the oldest of the inter-denominational campus ministries. The direct descendant of Inter-Varsity Fellowship (now Universities and Colleges Christian Fellowship) in England, IVCF traces its roots and name to the religious revival among English students at Cambridge in the 1870s. The organization was legally incorporated in the United States in 1941 as a distinctively evangelical campus ministry and now has headquarters in Madison, Wisconsin. Its president is John W. Alexander, former chairperson of the department of geography at the University of Wisconsin, Madison, and a nonjudgmental believer in biblical inerrancy. (He is much more conservative in almost every way than his regional directors.)

Each member of the IVCF staff and corporation must affirm his or her commitment to the organization's statement of faith, which is identical to that of The Theological Students Fellowship. Most staff members have not attended seminary. Like their Crusade counterparts, they too must raise their own support for ministry. IVCF staffers, however, facilitate and advise (rather than direct) the IVCF chapters on over 800 campuses, which are essentially student controlled. These chapters meet weekly for Bible study, prayer, and fellowship. Evangelism in IVCF is generally conducted on a one-to-one, long-term, friendship basis. Its style runs counter to Crusade's aggressive evangelism.

IVCF has several conference centers throughout the United States, and schedules over 100 weekend gatherings and sundry summer training programs for students and staff each year. It promotes a (rather ineffective) ministry to faculty on college and university campuses, and has a separate Nurses Christian Fellowship. *HIS* magazine, edited by Linda Doll and published monthly during the school year, represents a fairly moderate expression of left evangelical views. InterVarsity Press publishes popular and scholarly books of evangelical conviction, an increasing number of which can be rightly termed politically and socially radical. Both *HIS* and InterVarsity Press are located in Downers Grove, Illinois. Closely associated with, but independent of, IVCF is the chain of Logos bookstores, based in Ann Arbor, Michigan, and situated in major university communities throughout the country. These stores provide an alternative to the average conservative Christian bookstores by offering scholarly and popular religious publications of the entire theological spectrum, not just the evangelical right and center.

IVCF's biggest claim to fame, however, is its triennial missionary convention held on the campus of the University of Illinois at Urbana. Eminent evangelical leaders from many different countries and cultural perspectives are recruited as speakers to encourage the students in attendance to consider world and home mission work as a vocation. Urbana '76 emphasized Third World concerns and was attended by over 17,000 people, mostly college and university students. (United Presbyterians, numbering over 1000, and United Methodists, nearly 800 in attendance, represented the largest denominational groupings.)

Theologically, Inter-Varsity Christian Fellowship was born in the ethos of British evangelical rationalism, but it now represents a wide diversity of positions characteristic of the evangelical left. Today's IVCF students are not nearly as activist as those who attended Urbana '70 (the student mood in the wider culture has changed too), but chapter, area, and regional staff try hard (often unsuccessfully) to instill a social conscience in their generally apathetic student leaders. Local chapters of IVCF are mainly white, with a significant minority of Asian-Americans, however. Women function both as chapter officers and as staff persons with all the rights and responsibilities of their male counterparts.

IVCF in the United States (and more so in Canada) is becoming an increasingly mainline student movement and, in a sense, is replacing the denominational Protestant and ecumenical campus ministries that no longer attract significant numbers of students. There are no legalistic lifestyle expectations on IVCF staff and students. They enjoy having a good time—even if it involves social dancing and having a few drinks. Some chapters, however, tend to be more liberal than others, theologically and culturally, varying from campus to campus and from region to region. IVCF in the Midwest, near headquarters, for instance, tends to be far more conservative than IVCF in the Pacific Northwest. When you've seen one chapter or region, you haven't seen them all.

Youth for Christ

At the level of ministry to high school (and, in one instance, junior high school) youth, two organizations of the evangelical left are most important. Youth for Christ International (YFC) is the first and the best known. Founded in 1944, with Torrey Johnson as its first president, YFC quickly became a worldwide movement. Billy Graham, who joined the organization in 1944, was its first full-time worker, preaching at YFC's revivalistic Saturday evening rallies. With headquarters in Wheaton, Illinois, this organization now ministers to teenagers in 39 nations of the world, including approximately 1250 high schools in the United States. It has about 800 full-time staff members, who begin their training as interns, for at least a year, raising their own support of $650 per month.

The major ministries of YFC are its monthly award-winning and very

sophisticated magazine, *Campus Life*. Campus Life is also the designation for the high school ministry in cities and suburbs that consists of
campus-oriented clubs, meeting weekly and designed for evangelism
"through teen events and staff to teen relationships." Youth Guidance is
a wide-ranging ministry with a variety of programs to reach out to troubled youth, including delinquents.

In its theological thrust and cultural attitudes, YFC would hardly be
recognized today by those who attended its rallies in the 40s, 50s, and
early 60s but have had no contact with the organization since then. The
United States movement's president, Jay Kesler, is a very progressive
thinker and leader. YFC's understanding of evangelism and ministry is
based upon a desire to "achieve maximum influence. It must have potential for multiplication and be person centered. It must be characterized by
a Spirit-led boldness, a long term patience, responsibility, and fiscal
trustworthiness." (Indeed, YFC, like Campus Crusade for Christ, has
been approved for charitable solicitation purposes by the Council of
Better Business Bureaus.)[1]

Young Life

The second very important (and sometimes downright radical) left
evangelical organization of ministry to high school (and junior high
school) age youth is The Young Life Campaign in Colorado Springs.
Young Life was founded in 1941 by Jim Rayburn, a Presbyterian minister in Dallas, for the express purpose of reaching out to high school age
people who had dropped out of (or were never part of) the church. This remains the movement's chief intention today.

Each week during the school year, some 67,000 young people are
involved in Young Life clubs, coordinated by over 425 full-time field
staff. In one-hour informal livingroom sessions, these people "come
together for fun, fellowship, singing, and a talk by the leader in comfortable everyday language about Jesus Christ and His reality in today's
struggles." Headed by Robert Mitchell as executive director, Young Life
recently made the news by hiring as a ranking officer Jeb Magruder of
Watergate fame. Magruder was converted through the influence of Louis
Evans, Jr., senior minister of the National Presbyterian Church in Washington, D.C., and Senator Mark Hatfield.

With an annual overall budget of about $15 million, Young Life also
operates summer, weekend, and holiday camps in many areas throughout

the country. It crosses the Catholic–Protestant dividing line at every level, and bridges the cultural gaps between black and white, Jew and Gentile, male and female, adult and adolescent. In 1974 Young Life established an Office of Urban Affairs in Chicago, and Urban Young Life staffers now seek to stand alongside oppressed city youngsters, largely blacks and other minorities, in some 20 urban centers of the United States. It places special emphasis on advocacy, justice issues, and job referral, in addition to more traditional spiritual and relational concerns.

Theologically, Young Life is a movement that is not at all interested in the niceties of doctrinal orthodoxy. Its ministry represents a major "fleshing out" of relational theology. Young Life has such a low profile that it is almost invisible as an organization. The movement is strongly attracted to the evangelical left, its leaders, theology, and social concerns. For twenty years Young Life has operated its own institute in Colorado for training leadership. Core courses are offered every summer in disciplines such as ethics, philosophy of religion, church history, theology, and biblical studies. Paul K. Jewett and Lewis B. Smedes are prominent instructors at the institute.

Youth Specialties

One of the most important marks of Christian maturity, I feel, is the willingness to be self-critical—and beyond that, even, the ability to laugh both at oneself and that which one represents. Traditionally, few evangelicals have displayed these qualities to any degree at all. They have been dead serious both as individuals and as religious leaders. But Youth Specialties (San Diego, California), founded in 1969, is an organization for the training of ordained youth ministers and lay leaders that operates with a sense of humor possibly unmatched in the religious world today.

Presently, over 10,000 youth ministers throughout the United States receive services and resources from this growing organization. Its close contact with numerous and varied ministries keeps Youth Specialties' staff on the cutting edge of the national youth scene. The organization itself publishes the popular *Ideas* series, a periodical encyclopedia of youth ministry ideas and resources. Youth Specialties also has a unique training program that takes its staff and one nationally known Christian leader across the country to present seminars geared to help youth workers better understand the theology, philosophy, function, and program of their own ministry. It also conducts a growing tape ministry, distributing a wide variety of cassette tapes relating to the topics of Bible study, youth ministry, Christian living, and cultural programs. Speakers include Earl Palmer, Vernon Grounds, Jay Kesler, Robert Boyd Munger, Bill Pannell, and black evangelist Tom Skinner. Youth Specialties' National Youth Workers Convention is a four-day conference held annually in October that features dozens of highly respected experts in youth work.

This very nontraditional organization was created by Wayne Rice and Mike Yaconelli, both of whom had served with YFC on the local and national levels and helped develop the Campus Life ministry. Denny Rydberg later joined the staff after serving as youth minister at two West Coast Presbyterian churches. Although Youth Specialties' staff hate to be categorized and labeled theologically, they and their organization fit well into the evangelical left, as witnessed to in *The Wittenburg Door,* their bimonthly magazine. *The Wittenburg Door* contains media reviews, editorials, regular features, humorous satire (very funny indeed), and in-depth interviews, including apocalyptic author Hal Lindsey (June–July 1971), Jay Kesler (April–May 1972), Robert H. Schuller (June–July 1975), Marabel Morgan (August–September 1975), Martin E. Marty (December 1975–January 1976), Earl Palmer (February–March 1976), Harvey Cox (August–September 1976), Maggie Kuhn of the Gray Panthers (December 1976–January 1977), and Bill Bright (February–March 1977).

The *Door* gives its coveted "green weenie" ("loser of the month") award to Christian personalities on a regular basis, thus providing recognition to individuals with absurd or questionable ideas and practices from a Christian perspective. For example, Patricia French won the award in the April–May 1976 issue—"photographed in her famous 'let-it-all hang-out' pose complete with ultra mini skirt, special see-through evening gown and ravishing 'truck-stop waitress' hairstyle." Robert H. Schuller won it in the December 1976–January 1977 issue for his money-raising campaign for the 14-million-dollar Crystal Cathedral in Garden Grove; Ray Batema, pastor of Central Baptist Church in Pomona, California, in the December 1975–January 1976 issue, for his sermon on "Feeding 5000" with "free fishburgers and drink to all who attend"; and Paul B. Tinlin, an Assemblies of God pastor in Hoffman Estates, Illinois, in the same issue, for his favoring of broadcasting executions of convicted murderers on prime-time television as "an unbeatable shock method" to help stop crime.

Liberal Protestant ministers and laity who still criticize these growing left evangelical youth ministry organizations would do well to examine what their own churches and denominations are doing as an alternative. Witness the dramatic decline in youthful members and participants in recent years to the point that the United Church of Christ, for instance, now has an average age among its membership of 57, and a median age of 50.

NEW FORMS OF WITNESS

Many will remember the highly liturgical underground church that served the "movement" (usually younger) radicals of the 60s, who charged their parent Catholic and liberal Protestant churches with hypocrisy in worship, lifestyle, and attitude toward justice issues. The underground church had died by the 70s, but evangelicals and charismatics picked up the ball and began forming their own new models of Christian witness and celebration, again, in reaction to older hypocritical forms utilized this time by the evangelical establishment. The Jesus movement itself provided a catalyst for the changing mood regarding worship and witness among younger evangelicals, particularly with its new music, spontaneity, and willingness to accept nonconformists in dress and behavior. There now exist numerous experimental churches and communities, some distinctively evangelical in character; others mixed evangelical and mainline Protestant (the activist Church of the Savior in Washington, D.C., for example); still others distinctively charismatic (the communitarian Episcopal Church of the Redeemer in Houston, for instance). Two especially prominent distinctively evangelical models of Christian celebration and witness in this category are L'Abri Fellowship in Huemoz, an Alpine village near Lausanne, Switzerland (which has profoundly influenced many younger evangelicals in the United States), and LaSalle Street Church in Chicago. Both of these groups operate independently of denominational control, and both, in some way, try to integrate biblical faith with social concern.

L'Abri Fellowship

L'Abri was established in 1955 by Francis Schaeffer and Edith Schaeffer. Their purpose was to provide an accepting atmosphere for students, scholars, and other seekers from around the world to study Scripture and theology within a context of warm Christian fellowship and worship.

L'Abri (a French word meaning *shelter*) is located in a very beautiful Alpine setting, where the Schaeffers have built a number of chalets for study, lodging, and entertainment. All serious seekers after truth are welcome, and guests regularly include atheists, agnostics, Catholics, Protestant liberals, Hindus, Buddhists, and traditional and nontraditional evangelicals. Francis Schaeffer, a culture critic widely admired in evangelical circles, tries in his writing and teaching to relate rational evangelical orthodoxy (with a presuppositional approach to theistic argumentation) to contemporary culture and philosophical problems.

Schaeffer's early books, *The God Who Is There* and *Escape from Reason*, and many of his later ones too, have been extremely influential among younger evangelicals in helping them have and express a reason for their faith. Both of the Schaeffers have also assisted these young Christians to develop an appreciation for the best products of the wider culture—art, literature, and music, among them—traditionally ignored by the American evangelical community as a whole.

Francis and Edith Schaeffer, to their credit, have sought in their community at L'Abri to "show forth, in our life and work, the existence of God." Behind that vocation rests Francis' apologetics, based on three overriding principles he and Edith affirm boldly:

1. The full doctrinal position of historic Christianity must be clearly maintained [i.e., Old Princeton orthodoxy].
2. Every honest question must be given an honest answer. It is unbiblical for anyone to say, "just believe" [hence Christian apologetics is an important discipline].
3. There must be an individual and corporate exhibition that God exists in our century, in order to show that historic Christianity is more than just a superior dialectic or a better point of psychological integration [thus L'Abri].[2]

Like Carl F. H. Henry, Schaeffer distrusts any existential posture or any stance in which subjective experience is used to legitimate religious truth, so he views both neo-orthodoxy and charismatic renewal with suspicion. In recent years, as we have seen already, he has led the intellectual contingent who insist that biblical inerrancy is the evangelical watershed. In so doing, however, Schaeffer has alienated many of his evangelical sisters and brothers who once felt the warmth, openness, and total acceptance of L'Abri and appropriated them in their own lives and ministries but are now confused by the contradiction between the atmosphere at

L'Abri and Schaeffer's seemingly closed intellectual and relational posture toward those who reject inerrancy.

LaSalle Street Church

LaSalle Street Church, once a mission of Moody Church in Chicago until the former became too radical, is the Chicago area's most creative and innovative activist congregation of the evangelical left. Located in a dangerous part of the inner city where the church's senior minister himself has been mugged, LaSalle Street Church called Bill Leslie to lead its ministry in 1961. The social liberation movements of the 60s were to have a great impact on the congregation. By 1965 Leslie and his young adult leadership decided unequivocally that the church must be "committed to God through the redemptive work of Christ, bound to one another in a caring body of believers, and joined together in a whole-person ministry to people in the community."[3] Throughout the late 60s and the 70s, these principles have been adhered to faithfully. LaSalle Street Church now has a large staff of clergy and lay leaders, a counseling center, a legal aid and advocacy office, a tutoring and recreation program for (mostly black) children and older youth, community meals for senior citizens, a Logos bookstore with its own ministry, and a full schedule of worship, Bible and theological study, fellowship groups, and social action more generally.

The church itself tends to be attended by left-leaning younger Christians, many of whom commute from a long distance (Wheaton College, for example). Mainly white, its membership consists of upper-middle-class activists and intellectuals. In 1972 sociologist David Moberg of Marquette University in Milwaukee conducted an in-depth survey of members, regular attenders, and visitors to LaSalle Street Church, with the following results: It is indeed a young congregation (61 percent under 25 years of age; 80 percent under 35); two-thirds (now one-third) single; well educated (51 percent college or university graduates; 25 percent with some graduate school education); and theologically conservative but politically liberal (only 25 out of 252 who completed the questionnaire termed themselves theologically liberal). Most of those surveyed "strongly agreed" or "agreed" that the church should continue to express social concern for individuals "even if they reject the call to salvation."[4]

It must be noted at this point that of these two distinctively evangelical models of Christian witness and clebration, only one—LaSalle Street

Church—can legitimately be called an integral part of the evangelical left. However, L'Abri Fellowship has been very influential in shaping the lives of many who now identify with left evangelical concerns.

WORLD MISSION AND EVANGELISM

We have already taken a look at the evangelistic techniques of prominent left evangelical campus and youth ministry organizations. Evangelism within the evangelical left as a whole is generally not very aggressive, though it is persistent. Its major concern is not quick conversions or getting the maximum number of souls saved in the shortest period of time. Evangelism is viewed as holistic, in that it focuses on meeting the needs of the whole person—physical, economic, social, and intellectual, as well as spiritual. The proclamation and demonstration of the Gospel in word and deed are integrally related, and most of the time evangelism has to do with long-term relationships, friendship, lifestyle, and listening as well as speaking. Mission, as an outgrowth of the evangelistic mandate, is also understood as having to do with the total needs of all unreached people throughout the world. Right doctrine is best expressed in service, in right practice; and the search for social justice ("liberation") and evangelism may be distinguished from each other, but they cannot be separated.

World Vision International

One of the most important organizations for world mission and evangelism aligned with the evangelical left, at points at least, is World Vision International (Monrovia, California), founded in 1950 by the venerable Bob Pierce to care for Korean War orphans. Since then it has grown to a ministry spanning the globe in more than 40 countries, with an annual budget of more than $20 million. World Vision is concerned with ministering to children and families through orphanages, schools, and family aid programs. It provides emergency aid in food, medical assistance, and immediate housing for people suffering as a result of war or natural disasters. The organization is very much interested in self-development, and helps people produce adequate nourishment, earn a decent income, and plan for survival and growth. World Vision also engages in pastoral and lay leadership training. Through MARC (Missions Advance Research and Communications), headed by Ed Dayton, it gathers statistics on major and minor mission fields for the use of mission boards and other organizations and individuals—physical features; population growth, density, and distribution; languages; government; economy; and religion, all updated on a regular basis. (In the monthly *World Vision* magazine, MARC publishes its "facts of a field" articles, providing statistics in condensed form, a brief sketch of the field's history, the current status of Christianity in the field, and present mission work being conducted there.) The depth and quality of this service is probably unique.

World Vision, especially MARC, works closely with Fuller Seminary's School of World Mission. It now receives a greater percentage of its contributions (only 5 percent of which goes to administration) from members of mainline Protestant churches than from members of distinctively evangelical denominations who often prefer the NAE's World Relief Commission or other more conservative organizations. Like Campus Crusade for Christ and Youth for Christ, World Vision is also approved by the Council of Better Business Bureaus.[5] Recently the organization has been directing increased attention to the world hunger crisis. Its president, W. Stanley Mooneyham, has written a moving book on the problem, *What Do You Say to a Hungry World?*, and has hosted a major television special on the issue. (World Vision's television efforts as a whole have been particularly successful in raising money for world relief.)

In many ways World Vision International is not a radical kind of ministry. In public relations and in the lifestyles of its chief executives, the organization shows its middle-class stripes (albeit tempered by idealism). Yet its ministries in the field are conducted ecumenically, without imposing a faith requirement as the price of service.

Liberation Theology

It should be mentioned at this point that the true nonpacifist radicals within the broader evangelical left are emerging in Central and South America. Their understanding of world mission and evangelism is reflected increasingly in the "liberation theology" that has grown out of the concrete experience of oppression suffered by the majority of Latin Americans, Protestant, Catholic, and non-Christian alike. Liberation theology has been represented by the works of a number of Latin American theologians, including Gustavo Gutierrez, Catholic author of the groundbreaking *A Theology of Liberation,* Jose P. Miranda, Rubem Alves, Juan Luis Segundo, and Jose Miguez Bonino, a president of the World Council of Churches, and an evangelical himself.

Liberation theology is a contemporary response to oppressive economic and political situations that seem totally insensitive to peaceful attempts at change. Thus it condones implicitly or explicitly the use of violence to facilitate revolution. Liberation theologians view their people as the heirs of the Exodus, counterparts of Israel in Egypt. God is delivering his people out of the bondage of political and economic oppression of right-wing military dictatorships in Latin America into socialism. First, these theologians repudiate the *method* of traditional European and North American theology, with its underlying assumption of the Greek (versus revolutionary and biblical) epistemological split between truth and practice. This method is to be replaced by an understanding of theology as critical reflection on praxis, that is, reflection within and upon the process of actual *engagement* in the struggle for liberation. Second, they believe that the way must be opened for the appropriation of sociopolitical analysis in theology as well as in Christian practice to secure and concretize Christian engagement in the liberation process. To a greater or lesser degree (depending on the theologian), Marxist analysis is employed to do just that. Third, liberation theologians believe that there must be the development of an intrinsic relationship between sin, salvation, and the Kingdom of God on the one hand, and the historical process and struggle for sociopolitical liberation on the other. Active involvement in our world precedes knowledge. Revelation comes out of obedience, and truth does not mirror the world passively; it is, rather, an active force transforming it.[6]

In addition to Miguez Bonino, a number of other leading Latin American evangelicals now affirm (though not uncritically) both liberation theology in general and the possibility of Marxist–Christian cooperation in working for social justice and political change in particular. Notable among them are Samuel Escobar,[7] René Padilla, and Orlando Costas, author of *The Church and Its Mission: A Shattering Critique from the Third World*, and a United Church of Christ missionary supported to direct the Latin American Evangelical Center for Pastoral Studies in San Jose, Costa Rica. They are joined by the faculty of the evangelical and charismatic Seminario Biblico Latinoamericano, also in San Jose,[8] and a number of national student movements affiliated with the International

Fellowship of Evangelical Students (such as the Asociacion Biblica Universitaria Argentina). To be sure, North American conservative evangelicals are greatly alarmed by this trend.

Gene Thomas and "Christian Psychotherapy"

Finally in this context, we should mention one new style of evangelism conducted in Boulder, Colorado, by United Presbyterian businessman Gene Thomas, a former Inter-Varsity staffer who still travels the IVCF lecture circuit in the United States and Canada. Gene Thomas and his wife Gerri began ministering to the counterculture in Boulder during its heyday in the 60s. Each Sunday evening their home is filled with more than 150 diverse people—millionaires, street people, students, professors, the mentally and emotionally disturbed—who come for Gene's Bible teaching and for fellowship. During the 60s, Gene and Gerri Thomas provided nightly dinners for about 250 at a vacant fraternity house, and they now run a telephone-answering service, laundry, gas station, stained glass company, and painting service in which they employ "nonproductive" people—drug addicts, "crazies," the mentally retarded, exfelons, and other outcasts—as part their rehabilitative program of Christian psychotherapy. The Thomases do not believe in mental institutions. Rather, it is their conviction that God intends mentally and emotionally handicapped people to be part of a family, the church, which, they feel, is uniquely equipped and constituted to serve them.

Gene Thomas has a radical vision of what evangelism is about. He uses a totally accepting, nonthreatening approach that centers on long-term personal relationships and Bible study. He focuses on the parables and other teachings of Jesus in the Synoptic Gospels (particularly the hard sayings of Jesus—the radical ones). Christians are followers of Jesus, and conversion means *becoming* a follower of Jesus. The old, stereotyped, and culturally loaded vocabulary of traditional evangelicalism is avoided insofar as possible.

Gene's evangelism is part of his whole program in Christian psychotherapy, which seeks to meet the basic needs of people who come to him for help. "First, you need a friend," says Thomas. "That friend has to know quite a bit about you, really like you, and see you every day. Second, you need a group of about eight to ten others who know you pretty well, and would go to bat for you. And third, you need another

40 to 50 people who at least know you superficially and give you good vibes.''

Next, Thomas feels that ''you need work, and anything is better than nothing. It must involve some responsibility and feeling of accomplishment.'' Hence the businesses Thomas oversees and uses to employ nonproductive people (who ultimately *do* produce). ''You also need a good living situation,'' he declares. Sometimes he offers his own home; but more often, Gene, Gerri, and their colleagues help arrange more permanent accommodations. A person also needs structure, according to Thomas. This means doing something each day, including work or appointments or social obligations. In that context, discipline is important, ''Look for a job from 9 to 5, then come back for dinner. If you don't look for a job, no dinner.'' Finally, people need counseling and a purpose in life. Here is where Gene brings in his Bible teaching and answers religious questions. One of his creations is ''Bible study for pagans,'' an ongoing study group for ''bikers,'' go-go dancers, prostitutes, and the like. Participants are urged to read the Gospels and respond to what ''hits them between the eyes.'' A leader provides direction. Gene often relates how he once asked one of the members of this group, ''Are you still reading your Bible?'' and got the reply, ''Yeah, the son-of-a-bitch is in my back pocket.'' Thomas is able to reach the kind of person who, confronted by the typical evangelist, says, ''Don't give me that Bible shit!''

Gene and Gerri Thomas are also known for having had, at an earlier period in their lives, ''evangelistic cocktail parties,'' to which were invited 95 ''pagans,'' say, and 5 Christians. This provided a nonthreatening atmosphere for secular professionals such as lawyers, physicians, business people, and professors—in a context they understood and appreciated. (''Followers of Jesus are in the minority here, just like in the world,'' says Gene.)

Obviously, such evangelistic techniques as the Thomases have utilized are shocking to most conservative evangelicals. Yet these methods have allowed Gene and Gerri to reach people who would never be positively influenced in any other way. Furthermore, their evangelism, conducted in the context of their own community, enables them to provide hurting individuals with the love, friendship, and support they need on the road back to health.[9]

9

Changing Cultural Attitudes

As we have seen, the wider culture has had a profound impact on the evangelical movement as a whole during the last decade. This influence has been especially significant on the evangelical left. Left evangelicals are now responding affirmatively to the widespread call for simpler living, showing an increasing appreciation for secular culture, and no longer viewing as binding the traditional evangelical taboos. Evangelicals of the left have made their peace with science, and many have become feminists. They have discovered the pleasure of sex, and have begun to question the *priority* of the nuclear family and explore alternative expressions of family life and sexuality. Furthermore, evangelicals of the left know that they are not the *only* Christians, and many of them have become avowedly ecumenical both in word and in deed.

Left evangelicals who were part of the counterculture of the 60s have brought with them a continuing interest in and commitment to community, expressed often and radically in voluntary poverty and collective ownership of their worldly goods. Some of the most visible radical evangelicals live in urban or rural communes or collectives.

THE CALL TO SIMPLER LIFESTYLES

Walter Hearn and Ginny Hearn are exemplary of left evangelicals who have adopted a simple lifestyle "somewhere between the rich and the radical, the weak and the strong, the fat and the lean." In 1971, at the age of 45, Walter was a research scientist and tenured professor at Iowa State

University at Ames. In 1972 he dropped out of the system. "I wanted to simplify my life along with my work, to find a 'life-work' of wholeness. I hadn't yet thought of simple living as a Christian obligation in the light of economic injustice, but I was beginning to see it as an ecological necessity."

Walter wanted to become a full-time writer. His wife, Ginny, is an experienced editor who once worked for Inter-Varsity's *HIS* magazine. As a professor, Walter had published scientific papers, book reviews, magazine articles, and chapters in books, some of them relating to his keen interest in the relationship of science to Christian faith. But he was also well aware of the great difficulty of earning a living through writing alone. In addition, Walter questioned his role as a teacher of future scientists. "Is it really society's needs that demand the training of more scientists in our image—or is it the demands of our own egos?" He began to question his Christian witness at Iowa State, noting that "I had left my mark on the place, trying to humanize the bureaucracy in various ways, and realized I could make a new kind of contribution simply by resigning. My department could replace me with a woman or a black, or at least with some young Ph.D. hungry for work in a tight job market." Walter also felt that with the depletion of natural resources and the rampant consumerism of Americans at the expense of the Third World, adopting a simpler lifestyle seemed an attractive option for him and his family. He wished to develop a more creative work-sharing relationship and egalitarian marriage with Ginny. "We wanted to work together at major tasks, to share a profession. It seemed clear that I could enter her profession [editing and writing] more easily than she could enter mine [scientific research]."

Given the adventurous spirit both of them had developed over the years—and their savings—they took their family to Berkeley, California, where Walter had taught for a while. They bought a large home, opened it up to students and transients (like Gene and Gerri Thomas, the Hearns regard hospitality as a Christian obligation), and, for the first few years, found themselves in a zero income tax bracket. Walter and Ginny learned how to be good scavangers for used clothing and furniture. His trips across Berkeley to "gather manna" have become famous. (Walter picks up discarded produce and other food at local markets, "recycles" it—he *is* a biochemist—and, with Ginny, cooks it so that nobody knows the difference.) Walter now edits the newsletter of the American Scientific Affiliation, and Ginny is copy editor of *Rādix* newspaper in Berkeley. Both of them have edited over 50 books for evangelical and secular publishers, and are active board members of New College, Berkeley, an emerging graduate school of theology, scheduled to open in the summer of 1978, to train Christian laity—modeled after Regent College.

The Hearns are finally earning an income again. A good deal of their time is still spent on hospitality, and both of them are working in various ways "to change the sexist patterns in church and society" (Ginny is coordinator of the East Bay Evangelical Women's Caucus). An article about their "journey toward simplicity" appeared in 1975 in the Los Angeles Times,[1] and was reprinted in *Moneysworth* (March 15, 1976) and a number of other national newspapers. Despite the title of the article ("Ph.D. Scrounges for a Living"), Walter insists that what they have done is not nearly as revolutionary as it may seem.

> After all, we have preserved our family structure, are paying off a mortgage, still have some savings and a car, work for the "establishment" whenever we can get free-lance editorial work from a publishing house, and are relatively dispassionate about politics. . . . I doubt that in the eyes of some we could ever become poor enough or radical enough to "escape the middle class." I'm not even sure I want to.

Walter and Ginny Hearn know that there is "a lot of room between feeling that we can't make any significant changes in the system and feeling that we have to change everything."[2]

APPRECIATING THE FINE ARTS

We have noted the influence of Francis Schaeffer on younger evangelicals, in motivating them to read secular and nonevangelical religious literature critically, and to appreciate good music and art, something often neglected by their culture-rejecting forebears. Credit can also be given to evangelical colleges where the best secular art, music, and literature have been emphasized in teaching more and more over the last decade or so. For several years, in its biweekly "Refiner's Fire" column, *Christianity Today* has treated the contemporary cultural contribution of writers, artists, and musicians with sophistication and often with sympathy. Consider, for instance, its knowledgeable assessment of folk-rock hero Bob Dylan (December 3, 1976); novelist Saul Bellow (January 21, 1977); artist Andrew Wyeth (February 4, 1977); novelist John Gardner and black rock musician Stevie Wonder (February 18, 1977); and the television series "Serpico," and mystery author Dorothy L. Sayers in a lead story (March 4, 1977). Reviews of secular bestsellers and movies (even R-rated ones) are regular features of *Vanguard, Sojourners,* and *Radix.*

Evangelical teenagers have listened to rock music faithfully (to the chagrin of their parents) from the emergence of the late Elvis Presley and Pat Boone (himself a charismatic) in the 50s, and have, in more recent years, acted out rock rhythms in dancing. But it was the Jesus movement itself that really brought the wider culture and the counterculture of the 60s to younger evangelicals as a whole. Although participants in that movement Christianized rock ("filigreed" it with Jesus), they always kept in touch with the latest trends and performers in secular rock. Evangelical artists like Pat Boone, Cliff Richard (in England), country singer-composer Johnny Cash (now a pentecostal), and B. J. Thomas have never fully discarded in their concerts the earthy and erotic themes and rhythms of secular rock (always present in black Gospel music); nor have Christian rock's avant-garde, performers like Larry Norman and John Fischer, producers like Paul Baker of Word, Incorporated, and critics like Steve Turner of *Rolling Stone*. Indeed, rock is inherently a form of music that made its way by outrage against taboo, and there are no taboos left. It is profoundly significant that evangelicals, even the more conservative among them, have accepted the rock mode. This acceptance, obviously, indicates a further chapter in the death of self-denial and world rejection among them.

ABANDONING REVIVALISTIC TABOOS

An increasing number of evangelicals—left, center and right—no longer consider the traditional revivalistic taboos to be mandatory. When young people were converted in the Jesus movement, many of them simply did not give up their former habits, practices, and cultural attitudes—drinking, smoking, and characteristic dress and language. They only modified them. Evangelicals often discovered the pleasure of alcohol and tobacco while studying and traveling in Europe, where the typical revivalistic taboos do not function among local evangelical and charismatic Christians. Young evangelicals drink, but so do conservative evangelicals like Hal Lindsey and John Warwick Montgomery (who is a member of the International Wine and Food Society). Many young evangelicals smoke (a pipe, especially), but so does Jacob Preus, president of The Lutheran Church—Missouri Synod. In addition, four-letter and other once-proscribed words are now common in the conversation of left evangelicals. This fact should not be surprising to anyone who had a ministry in the Jesus movement to street people and hippies and had to communicate with them in the language they understood. Such language had clearly been deleted from the earthy and highly controversial interview with John Lennon and Yoko Ono in the November 1972 issue of *Right On* (now *Rādix*), a Berkeley-based radical evangelical newspaper born in the Jesus movement. But in a pivotal editorial on true spirituality in the September—October 1973 issue of *The Other Side,* the magazine's radical evangelical editor legitimized the appropriateness of street and bathroom language when it describes succinctly and clearly that which the majority of people understand.

It should be said at this point, however, that left evangelicals do tend to be more moderate in their behavior in all these areas than their Protestant liberal, Roman Catholic, and secular counterparts. There is clearly less drunkenness among them, and they are generally reluctant to use drugs. But even marijuana, now virtually legal in some areas of the United States, is not as forbidden among young evangelicals as it once was. A few of them, particularly the intellectuals, do smoke it on occasion, despite the fact that dope smoking is still discouraged by leaders of the evangelical left as a whole.

PARTICIPATION IN SCIENTIFIC RESEARCH AND TEACHING

At present evangelicals are involved in all the major areas of scientific research and teaching, but the proportion of evangelicals is probably highest in the physical sciences, somewhat lower in the biological sciences, and lowest in the social sciences. There are a number of specialized organizations for scholarly discussion and fellowship among evangelicals in science, including the Christian Medical Society and the Christian Association for Psychological Studies. The most important association of left evangelical scientists is the ASA—the American Scientific Affiliation (Elgin, Illinois). It is countered on the right and center by the Creation Research Society (San Diego, California), formed in 1963, which accepts creation as a scientific fact and claims as mandatory Christian views a "young earth" and a sudden origin of life.[3]

The ASA is a fellowship of men and women of science that was founded originally in 1941 and had grown to a membership of over 2400 by 1975. Members must be engaged in some kind of broadly defined scientific work—mathematics, engineering, medicine, psychology, sociology, economics, and history, as well as physics, chemistry, biology, astronomy, and geology. The organization currently has 16 regional sections across the United States, and works closely with the Canadian Scientific and Christian Affiliation (Perth, Ontario), established only in 1973. The ASA publishes a bimonthly newsletter and a rather sophisticated scholarly quarterly, *Journal of the American Scientific Affiliation,* edited by Richard H. Bube, chairperson of the Department of Materials Science and Engineering at Stanford University. Bube was recently put out of the Evangelical Theological Society for refusing to sign its doctrinal statement. His book, *The Human Quest: A New Look at Science and Christian Faith,* is must reading for those who want to understand the evangelical left's attitude toward science in general. The ASA also has a book service to provide members with key works on science and faith, and holds its annual national meeting each August, with three days of symposia, papers, field trips, and worship.

The organization's statement of faith, signed by all members, states that "the Holy Scriptures are the inspired Word of God, the only unerring guide of faith and conduct," the limited inerrancy position. Although the ASA avoids taking a stand on divisive issues in the evangelical community at large, such as evolution, it is indeed clear that the majority of its present members believe in some form of theistic evolution, and affirm an "old" rather than "young" view of the earth.

EVANGELICAL FEMINISM

Evangelical feminism (or *biblical feminism,* as it is often called) is a product of the secular women's liberation movement of the late 60s and the 70s. The feminist movement has demonstrated that many (though not all) middle-class women do not have a sense of worth and dignity when their role in life is limited to childbearing and the confines of home and family. Being a feminist means having a social, political, and often religious analysis regarding the oppression of women as well as a desire to promote the welfare of *all* women. Evangelical feminists insist that traditional evangelical teachings about women and their role in church and society simply do not result in mature, adult discipleship. In criticizing these teachings, they appeal to a secular analysis of the social order.[4]

We have already seen that right and center evangelicals like Bill Gothard, Larry Christenson, and Marabel Morgan affirm the traditional subordination of women to men (in marriage, at least) by appealing to Scripture, taken literally. Former missionary and conservative evangelical author Elisabeth Elliot claims that the traditional man–woman relationship also reflects the submissive relationship of Christ to God. In *Let Me Be a Woman,* she suggests that a wife can find true freedom only by submitting to the authority of her husband, because in so doing she is really submitting to God himself. This does not mean that a married woman cannot work outside the home; but it does mean that she must always put the good of her husband and family ahead of her own. And if her career demands too much time in that respect, she must give it up. In 1976 the Commission on Theology and Church Relations of The Lutheran Church–Missouri Synod concluded that the synod ought to express "major reservations" about the Equal Rights Amendment (ERA) to the Constitution, stating that although women should be treated equally in the workplace, they must always submit to their husbands in marriage; and passage of the ERA—with its demand for unlimited equality for women—could affect the church's teachings on the matter adversely.[5] Such views appear to be shared by most center and right evangelical women and men, including Billy Graham and his wife, Ruth Bell Graham.

The roots of contemporary evangelical feminism—a movement within the evangelical left—can be traced back to Russell Prohl's book, *Woman in the Church* (Grand Rapids, Mich: Eerdmans, 1957). Then came freelance writer Letha Scanzoni's article in the February 1966 issue of *Eternity,* "Women's Place: Silence or Service?" advocating the ordination of women. Two years later she argued in the same magazine for the elevation of marriage to a partnership. In 1969 Scanzoni began corresponding with Nancy Hardesty, who was then teaching at Trinity College (Illinois), about the possibility of co-authoring a groundbreaking book on evangelical feminism—a work that was published finally in 1974 as *All We're Meant To Be: A Biblical Approach to Women's Liberation.* It was preceded by other articles on that issue, including Hardesty's pivotal "Women and Evangelical Christianity," in *The Cross and the Flag* (1972). Radical evangelicals were introduced to feminism when Sharon Gallagher became editor of *Right On* in 1973.

In November 1973 the signers of the Chicago Declaration acknowledged "that we have encouraged men to prideful domination and women to irresponsible passivity. So we call both men and women to mutual submission and active discipleship." (*Mutual submission* has been used by evangelical feminists as a more pious and Christian-sounding substitute for the word *equality*.) A follow-up Thanksgiving worship held in 1974 to implement the Chicago Declaration accomplished little, but the invited participants were introduced at that gathering to a new evangelical feminist monthly, *Daughters of Sarah* (Chicago), founded by Lucille Sider Dayton, which continues to supply readers with articles on feminism, bibliographies, and news of evangelical feminist activities. Since its inception the magazine has enjoyed an increasingly wide readership among both evangelicals and nonevangelicals.

In November 1975 an evangelical feminist conference was held in Washington, D.C. that attracted 360 participants from across the United States, including a high proportion of Presbyterians, Baptists, and Mennonites. The conference formally endorsed the ERA and established the Evangelical Women's Caucus (EWC), a grassroots consciousness-raising organization, with major chapters in Washington, D.C., Boston, Minneapolis, Los Angeles, and the San Francisco Bay Area, and smaller chapters in other cities. Possibly 2000–3000 women are active members of a chapter and/or receive EWC mailings.[6] Evangelical feminist news and views now appear regularly in radical evangelical magazines and newspapers like *Sojourners, Rādix,* and *The Other Side,* as well as *The Wittenburg Door, Faith at Work,* and some of the more conservative evangelical magazines.

By and large, evangelical feminists are white, upper-middle-class intellectuals and activists, students and professionals, both single and married, with a number of divorced people among them. (New black evangelicals, however, feel that the struggle against racism must take priority over feminist concerns.) The ideas of evangelical feminists are reminiscent of those of the early secular feminists in the modern movement. Theirs is a practical, task-oriented approach, concerned with the problems of career women and those who wish to be freed from the confines of housework, who affirm both egalitarian marriage and singleness as viable Christian options, and who support the ordination of women. They would fit well into a moderate wing of the National Organization of Women (NOW). The more radical evangelical feminists share some of the ideas of socialist feminists—their special interest in the poor, Third World and working-class women, and a critique of capitalism as a major oppressor of women. Few, if any, of the evangelical feminists at present have much in common with the sectarian, lesbian wing of radical feminism. Evangelical feminists in general, moreover, tend to be Christians first and feminists second. They have not yet made a religion of feminism.

Though all evangelical feminists end up essentially in the same place biblically, the more conservative group—Sharon Gallagher, Letha Scanzoni, and Nancy Hardesty, perhaps—stand on the principle that the Bible does not teach what it has been assumed to teach about the subordinate role of women in church and society. Rather, the male-dominated accepted interpretation of Scripture (''priestcraft,'' in Gallagher's opinion), has distorted our understanding of the word. When we get back to what Paul really meant, we shall see that he was a feminist in disguise. In *All We're Meant to Be,* Scanzoni and Hardesty use the ''analogy of faith'' method to deal with the Pauline (and other) passages in question:

> The biblical theologian does not build on isolated proof texts but first seeks the . . . major biblical statement on a given matter. . . . Passages which are theological and doctrinal in context are used to interpret those where the writer is dealing with practical local cultural problems. . . . [With the exception of Galatians 3:28, the ''major biblical statement'' on the matter] all of the references to women in the New Testament are contained in passages dealing with practical concerns about personal relationships or behavior in worship services (pp. 18, 19).

For evangelical feminists the three basic teachings pertinent to the biblical understanding of women are (1) the first creation account—Genesis 1:27—declaring that God created human beings, male *and* female, in his own image (thus God has both masculine *and* feminine qualities); (2) the revelation of the life of Jesus (he was a feminist in his treatment of women in a male chauvinist society[7]); and (3) Galatians 3:28: ''There is no such thing as Jew and Greek, slave and freeman, male and female; for you are all one person in Christ Jesus'' (NEB). The conservative group feels that the apparent contradictions in the Bible are just that—only apparent.[8]

The biblically radical group of evangelical feminists—Paul K. Jewett and Virginia Ramey Mollenkott, author of *Women, Men and the Bible*—argue simply that the New Testament conveys liberation for all people and was not intended to oppress modern women by imposing a first-century patriarchal structure on them. In *Man as Male and Female*, Jewett applies the analogy of faith principle differently from Scanzoni and Hardesty. He considers passages that appear to contradict the general foundational truths (major biblical statements) to be, in fact, contradictory. The particular statements are wrong, but the general statements are right. Furthermore, as we have seen, Jewett believes that Paul's teachings about women (except Galatians 3:28) were influenced both by his male-dominated culture and by rabbinic traditions representing no more than a time-bound authority, not applicable to later Christians in other cultures. When we discern the cultural conditioning of Scripture, we are also free to say that a writer, like Paul, may indeed be wrong at points. At least the authority of the writer's teaching (matters of faith and practice) may no longer be applicable. Because the conservatives' argument that Paul did not really mean what we thought he meant involves a strained and quite unconvincing exegesis, we can assume that the radicals' methodology will eventually become dominant in left evangelical circles.

It can be argued that evangelical feminism emerged, in part, at least, because of (1) the new exegesis and biblical criticism employed by evangelical scholars; (2) the increased interest in social ethics among evangelicals more generally; (3) and the new historical studies of prominent nineteenth-century evangelical women and men who were feminists. Most notable among scholars of this expression of feminism are Donald W. Dayton and Lucille Sider Dayton, who have published widely on the topic in scholarly and popular religious magazines. In *Discovering an Evangelical Heritage* (especially pp. 85–98), Donald W. Dayton argues that there are "evangelical roots of feminism" in the lives and work of nineteenth-century evangelical reformers, and that by and large the Wesleyan, holiness, Arminian tradition has been much more open to feminism than the Calvinist tradition (especially its "Old School" Presbyterian form) has been. Prominent among these early reformers were Charles G. Finney; Angelina Grimké and Sarah Grimké (Quaker abolitionists); Luther Lee (an early leader of The Wesleyan Church); Jonathan Blanchard; B. T. Roberts; A. J. Gordon (Baptist namesake of Gordon College and Gordon-Conwell Theological Seminary); William

Booth and Catherine Booth; Hannah Whitall Smith (author of the best-selling *The Christian's Secret of a Happy Life* —first published in 1888 — and a major force behind the British Keswick Conventions); Frances Willard of the Women's Christian Temperance Union; and Amanda Smith (the black Methodist evangelist and ex-slave who preached around the world).

But Ina J. Kau, in what is probably the first major study of contemporary evangelical feminism, feels that the Daytons have overstated the spiritual continuity between these nineteenth-century evangelical feminists and their modern counterparts. The former's feminism, she believes, was acted out in different ways and for different reasons.

> [N]ineteenth century women turned to a legitimate activity, church work, where they joined the church's struggle against the world. Their activities gave them experience and expertise which some of them used later in the emerging feminist struggle. But their initial plunge into active public life did not entail feminist sentiments. These women desired to do God's work as it was defined by the church.
>
> Present-day evangelical feminists operate in a different way. The majority of their leaders have, or are in the process of training for, active professional lives. They have also learned from the feminist movement to articulate the pain and struggle of those lives in a feminist way. They are seeking now to change the church's attitudes about women so that church doctrine will more nearly fit the reality of their lives.[9]

Kau suggests that contemporary left evangelicals, influenced by the secular women's liberation movement, decided to be feminists, *then* went to the Bible to legitimize their stance:

> The [evangelical] feminists did not carefully examine the biblical texts, consult theology books and their ministers, and then declare themselves feminists. Rather, there was something about the [secular] feminist articulation of what it means to be a woman in American society that seemed true to them. They took . . . a leap of faith, claiming to be feminists despite the teachings of their church. Their biblical and theological work came after this leap.[10]

She also claims that, despite their commitment to the full authority of the Bible, evangelical feminists share a traditionally liberal methodology in dealing with that authority. They emphasize the relativity of traditional orthodox doctrinal formulations, insist that personal experience can inform Christian social ethics, and believe that appropriate Christian behavior can be learned from the world as well as from the Bible and the church. [11] If Kau is correct, the emergence of evangelical feminism presents a clear example of the influence of trends in the wider culture on contemporary evangelical Christianity—a profound instance of the world setting the agenda for the church, rather than vice versa.

SEXUALITY

At present, and for the most part, left evangelicals share with center and right evangelicals a generally conservative attitude toward human sexuality and sexual behavior. For them sex is now good, clean fun in marriage, and they believe that the ideal of indissoluble marriage should be preserved. Divorce is not what God intended, but it is sometimes unavoidable—the lesser of two evils, perhaps. After divorce, remarriage, given the grace of God, is not only allowed, it is a right. Masturbation, too, is acceptable, though left evangelicals do see it as not easily fulfilling. Premarital intercourse is bad, and extramarital sexual relations are worse, but both can be forgiven. Pornography is not condoned, yet it does not warrant undue concern; there are worse evils to fight than pornography. Abortion is a "tragic choice," and promiscuity is always shunned because it reduces people to sex objects alone. Left evangelicals, much more than their right and center sisters and brothers, reject legalism in sexual matters. They are more likely to be tolerant of and compassionate with "offenders," and more willing to live with unanswered questions. Furthermore, if the situation warrants it, they are ready and willing to change their minds.

Lewis B. Smedes and Sex for Christians

Interestingly enough, evangelicals of the left have not yet written much about the general problem of human sexuality—as opposed to the specific issue of sexism—in our secular society. By mid-1977 at least, very few articles on human sexuality per se had appeared in young evangelical publications like *The Wittenburg Door, Radix, The Other Side,* and *Sojourners*—indicative, perhaps, of changing attitudes among left evangelicals not yet expressed publicly. However, Fuller Seminary Professor Lewis B. Smedes has produced a groundbreaking work for evangelicals on the topic, *Sex for Christians.* Unlike traditional evangelical approaches to sexuality, Smedes' book raises more questions than it answers. In treating sex for Christians, the author, an informed, pragmatic biblical ethicist, engages in a continuous dialogue with himself considering contemporary secular views of sexuality in comparison with his own. Debatable areas are given tentative direction or are simply left debatable. More than anything else, Smedes stresses the complexities inherent in real-life situations today, and the ambiguities of Scripture on many crucial issues.

The author of *Sex for Christians* begins his work by providing a thoroughly biblical theological setting for the ensuing discussion of specific problems and questions. He talks about sex for singles and marrieds (there is a sexual dimension to every relationship), and the recent phenomenon (influenced, obviously, by trends in the wider society) of Christian couples living together outside of formal marriage—"even if it has not been digested into the style of the Christian campus, it is likely to become a minority practice there eventually" (pp. 137–138). He treats the possibility of "responsible petting" for unmarried Christians, a beneficial practice that, he feels, need not lead naturally to intercourse. Petting, of course, has always been a debatable, though often allowed, practice among evangelicals as a whole, many of whom have been satisfied with the preservation of "technical virginity" involving anything but penetration. (It is interesting to note that some evangelicals, anyway, now regard oral sex as mere petting, not intercourse. Even Tim LaHaye and Beverly LaHaye, although they believe that handling another's genitals is "much too intimate for unmarried people," declare that oral sex may not be intercourse per se,[12] for biblical literalists, the only form of heretosexual sexual behavior explicitly condemned in Scripture.) But Smedes, while he is permissive about petting, does reduce technical virginity to the myth it really is, just as Harvey Cox had done in *The Secular City* in the mid-60s.

In discussing all aspects of premarital, nonmarital, and extramarital sex, Smedes most often opts for the traditional orthodox views, but he provides no easy formulas and urges his Christian readers to move beyond simplistic legalisms on the one hand and abstract ethical propositions on the other. In judging the sexual practices of others, Smedes makes the bold declaration that has not represented the characteristic stance of most center and right evangelicals: "Compassion should be the cutting edge of moral judgment and understanding the cutting edge of compassion" (p. 138).

By far the most controversial aspect of Smedes' book is his treatment of homosexuality. Although he clearly does not accept homosexual practice as morally commendable, he does argue for an "optimum homosexual morality" for the homosexual unable to remain celibate or become more heterosexual through extensive therapy: "Within his sexual experience, he ought to develop permanent associations with another person, associations in which respect and regard for the other as a person dominate their sexual relationship" (p. 73). (Many prominent right and center evangelicals and charismatics speak of homosexuals becoming heterosexual "overnight" after conversion. This possibility would be disputed even by Christian psychiatrists, and certainly by the multitudes of born-again gays who struggled with their homosexuality for years after conversion, without change. Such a dramatic alteration in sexual preference without therapy would be a miracle. And although miracles do occasionally happen, it is more likely that the sudden switch in sexual orientation occurred in people who were bisexual rather than truly homosexual, or represented a change from the *practice* of homosexuality to celibacy.) Smedes has become the first prominent evangelical theologian to allow for the possibility of *continued* homosexual practice among Christians when successful therapy or celibacy are not realistic options, arguing that homosexuals ("true inverts") are not accountable by reason of conscious choice for who they are but rather are the objects of divine grace, which accepts them as they are and, furthermore, allows them to come to live in sexual love in a Christian ethical way.

Homosexuality and Evangelicals Concerned

Conservative evangelical (and Southern Baptist) entertainer Anita Bryant's crusade against civil liberties for gays in the teaching profession, and her widespread backing by evangelicals generally, is a good example of the fact that center and right evangelicals are still in the forefront of antigay sentiment in the wider American society. They believe that, biblically speaking (citing Leviticus and the Pauline injunctions), homosexual practice is contrary to the will of God, that it threatens the nuclear family by providing bad role models to impressionable children, and that it is actually dangerous, because homosexuals (gay men, presumably) are especially prone to seduce young boys (psychologically and sociologically speaking, an incorrect assumption). This attitude—

reflecting in some cases the sexual identity confusion of those who hold it—demonstrates a total lack of understanding of the nature of homosexuality and the absence of compassion for those caught in the homosexual matrix. In recent years evangelicals have softened their stand by making the distinction between homosexual orientation (the condition) and practice (acting out the condition). Yet it is clear that most evangelicals, in concrete situations, fail to make that distinction. (Bryant, it seems, would deny civil liberties to both practicing and nonpracticing gays.) Nonpracticing lesbians and gay men, if they are known as such, are generally just as unwelcome in conservative evangelical churches as practicing gays, and they suffer the same social ostracism among evangelicals outside the church.

Left evangelicals, except members of the Evangelical Women's Caucus, who regularly discuss lesbianism as a feminist issue, have generally dodged the question of homosexuality. (We should note here that lesbianism has been less of a threat to Americans than male homosexuality. Until recently women were not considered to be as "sexual" as men, and are still not viewed as sexual aggressors. Thus, they are harmless. The public is much more willing to accept two women living together than two men. It is probably also true—in my opinion, at least—that the lesbian option is more a matter of conscious choice than male homosexuality, and is less primarily sexual in orientation. Many women become lesbians because they have simply been unable—not unwilling—to form a successful and fulfilling relationship with a man. With gay men, however, it is much more a matter of sheer physical attraction to members of their own sex.) In *The Young Evangelicals,* I suggested that the rejection of homosexuals by the church—the evangelical church, in particular—was the major reason for the founding in 1968 of a distinctively, but not exclusively, gay denomination, the Universal Fellowship of Metropolitan Community Churches (MCC), with headquarters in Los Angeles. Headed by Troy Perry, formerly a minister of the pentecostal Church of God of Prophecy, the MCC now has over 90 congregations, 100 ordained clergy, and 20,000 members, mostly in urban centers where gays tend to live. This denomination, though it will be surprising to some, is distinctively evangelical in character (with an increasing charismatic contingent as well). The MCC emphasizes both evangelism for conversion, in gay bars and other places frequented by homosexuals, and social action. Lately it has been stressing the fight against sexism in church and society. (Liberal Protestant gays, incidentally, are often put off by the MCC and its "rampant fundamentalism.")

More interesting for evangelicals, however, has been the establishment of a new advocacy organization, Evangelicals Concerned (EC), "a national task force of evangelicals concerned about the lack of preparation for dealing realistically with homosexuality in the evangelical community and about the implications of the Gospel in the lives of gay men and women." EC (Miami, Florida) was founded by Ralph Blair in 1976, and by the end of that year had grown to 12 chapters in a number of major cities of the United States, including New York, Boston, Atlanta, Chicago, Denver, Los Angeles, and San Francisco. Made up of lesbians, gay men, and sympathetic heterosexuals, the organization sponsors national conferences, consults with leaders in both the religious and secular communities, makes referrals for counseling, and publishes educational materials including *Contact,* its official newsletter. Local chapters hold meetings, rap sessions, and Bible studies. Ralph Blair himself is president of EC's board, director of the Homosexual Community Counseling Center (HCCC) in New York City, and a former Inter-Varsity staffer at the Universities of Pennsylvania and Delaware.

In their interpretation of Scripture, gay evangelicals employ essentially the same hermeneutical approach as Paul K. Jewett. The Bible is culturally conditioned, and not everything therein is eternally authoritative. Viewing the Old Testament, for instance, Blair says:

> The early Hebrews had to contend with what all ancient peoples had to contend: simple survival. Among the threats to survival such as war-like neighbors, droughts, floods, and the high incidence of infant mortality and maternal deaths, was any sexual activity which could not lead to conception. . . . There was a strong belief in Israel that after death, life continued in the children and in the children's children, and so on in a very corporate sense. Consequently, in preventing conception by engaging in homosexual activity, for example, the possibility of a continued community after death was ruled out.[13]

Looking at the New Testament and the rest of Scripture as a whole, gay evangelicals note that Jesus did not mention homosexuality at all, and Paul, in the few places he discusses it, referred to the "unnatural acts" of people with members of their own sex alone, since he did not understand that true homosexuals have a *natural* inclination toward members of their own sex. Gay evangelicals (and other Christians) contend that the morality of an act is determined by the intent of the actor, not the act itself —"Nothing is impure in itself" (Romans 14:14, NEB). Thus if homosexual practice is intended to express love as part of an ongoing, permanent relationship (evangelical gays do not openly condone promiscuity), rather than lust (viewing people as mere sex objects), it is morally good. (It is interesting to note at this point that the Jewett hermeneutic can easily make *relative* almost any of the ethical norms in Scripture. If evangelicals begin to use it extensively, we may discern the emergence of a "new morality"—informed by the Bible, but also by reason, experience, and the *situation* in question—in which they conclude, ultimately, that love is really the only absolute ethical norm.)

With the high visibility of the secular gay liberation movement, the continued growth of the MCC and Evangelicals Concerned, and the new-found sensual awareness of evangelicals as a whole, it will become harder and harder for gay evangelicals to remain celibate. Lesbians and gay men are to be found everywhere within the evangelical community, but still mostly in the "closet." (At Fuller Seminary acknowledged gays are encouraged to participate in therapy.) Right and center evangelicals may continue to say "no" to homosexual practice explicitly and homosexual orientation implicitly; but it seems likely that left evangelicals will finally come out closer to Ralph Blair than to Anita Bryant.

10

Getting Together: Left Evangelicals and Protestant Liberals

EVANGELICALS—THE NEW CHRISTIAN MAJORITY

Until recently Protestant liberalism has been the mainline—establishment—expression of Christianity in the United States. In the words of Martin E. Marty, "Mainline Protestanism, acculturated, accommodated, acclimatized, after experiencing almost artificial prosperity in the 1950s, suffered relative losses ever after."[1] Protestant liberals and their churches became so wedded to the dominant culture that their beliefs, values and behavior were virtually indistinguishable from that culture:

> [M]ainline churches always have the advantage that in years in which the official culture is secure and expansive, they are well off. . . . [but they] suffer in times of cultural crisis and disintegration, when they receive blame for what goes wrong in society but are bypassed when people look for new ways to achieve social identity and location. So they looked as good in the 1950s as they looked bad by the 1970s.[2]

Now, of course, evangelicalism, in its Protestant, Catholic, and charismatic forms, is really the mainline brand of American Christianity.

Most evangelicals view Protestant liberals as thoroughly secular humanists who utilize religious language to symbolize the same "natural" human experiences that psychologists and sociologists describe with the secular scientific vocabulary of their disciplines. Thus for liberals religious words like *born again, salvation, incarnation,* and *resurrection* take on a totally existential character, symbolizing changes in feeling, emotion, and even personality at the human level rather than a supernatural transformation initiated by God (*salvation* and *born again,* for instance), or genuinely historical events (*resurrection* and *incarnation,* for example). Similarly, most Protestant liberals consider evangelicals to be Bible-thumping, anti-intellectual bigots and ill-mannered fools. Both stereotypes are most often false. But not altogether so, and the fundamentalism of the right is matched by a left-liberal fundamentalism that—despite the supposed openness of liberalism—is just as narrow, defensive, bigoted, and unwilling to listen as the worst caricature of its strict conservative counterpart.

JOHN C. BENNETT ON LIBERALISM NOW

It is extremely difficult to adequately identify the theological characteristics of contemporary Protestant liberalism because it is such an amorphous and changing entity. However, we can be certain that the "old" liberalism that viewed Scripture merely as the record of the religious experiences of Israel, and Jesus as a moral example alone, is no longer pervasive or normative in seminaries or churches. Ethicist and theologian John C. Bennett, president emeritus of Union Theological Seminary in New York, feels that liberalism in the 70s ("neo-liberalism") has been unalterably influenced by neo-orthodoxy, even if neo-orthodoxy is now regarded as passé in liberal circles.

For Bennett liberalism affirms that "Christian life is a response to the revelation of which Christ is the center and the Bible is the record of that revelation. The Bible is not the revelation." Scripture, in his opinion, is "a creation of the church, but the church came into being in response to events recorded in the Bible."

According to Bennett, liberalism is, ideally, "open to truth from all sources." Modifications of the response to given revelation, which includes "general revelation," may come from "new knowledge," including biblical criticism, scientific research, the nuclear threat, and the contemporary experience of women and minorities as oppressed people. Furthermore, "Christian response to revelation is not an individualistic experience but it takes place within the Christian community.'' Churches give structure to that community, yet *all* religious institutions and many of their practices are dependent on their context.

In the eminent social ethicist's opinion, ''Christ is the normative revelation and the cross is the revelation both of God's forgiving love and of the consequences of sin. Christ is also the beginning of a new reality in human life and history.'' Both the new birth and the resurrection can be understood in relation to this reality. ''The tendency to consign non-Christians to eternal punishment is one of the worst abominations in Christian history.'' Non-Christians may be deprived of great gifts, but we cannot set limits on the grace of God and ''possible God-given compensations for such deprivation.'' Many people, according to Bennett, have rejected Christ because of the failure of the church. In this connection, the Marxist rejection of Christianity and of all religion, though a tragedy, must be seen as a judgment on the church.

Bennett then declares that, although ecumenical institutions have declined in popularity in recent years, Christ still wills the unity of all Christians, facilitated by the work of the Holy Spirit. Indeed, the church ought to put more emphasis on the work and experience of the Spirit by whom we get in touch with our feelings toward ourselves and one another. Heresy should be viewed as ''one-sidedness,'' not as error. The church needs to increase its tolerance and even loving affirmation of dissenters, and support religious liberty for all. Finally, and this is the ''ethical'' side of liberalism, the church knows that ''God revealed in Christ is on the side of the oppressed.'' It must, therefore, put less emphasis on order and obedience to authority and more on a commitment to ''transforming social justice.''[3]

This kind of liberal Protestant theology, obviously, betrays a shift to the right by a major, self-identified theological liberal, and it does represent an increasingly popular position held, to one degree or another, by his like-minded colleagues in the major ecumenical and denominational seminaries of liberal persuasion in the United States. (See Bennett's recent book, *The Radical Imperative*.) Interestingly enough, it comes at the same time that the evangelical left is identifying itself with the prominent theologians of neo-orthodoxy who informed Bennett's thinking so profoundly. Note, for instance, the evangelical left's view of Scripture as the witness to Christ—the center of revelation—its openness to new knowledge, its seeing the new birth as existential, its ecumenicity and tolerance of religious dissent, and its commitment to social justice over order and obedience to authority, and compare these traits and beliefs with the position espoused as theologically "liberal" by one of modern liberalism's greatest champions, John C. Bennett.

MOVING TOWARD ECUMENISM

The fundamentalist–modernist controversy left many, if not most, evangelicals outside the mainline Protestant denominations in which they and their forebears had been nurtured. Those who remained within those increasingly liberal denominations tended to keep to themselves, avoiding contact with nonevangelicals both within and outside their own churches. When Billy Graham began his ecumenical evangelism in the 50s—seeking the support and participation of mainline church leaders (Protestants and, later, Roman Catholics) for his crusades—the hardcore fundamentalists repudiated him for cooperating with "modernist unbelievers." But the evangelicals remained in his camp, convinced that this kind of ecumenical cooperation was itself evangelistic; liberal pastors and their congregations could be "reached for Christ."

Evangelicals of the left, however, have gone one step beyond a one-way ecumenism (getting the liberals saved). Not having participated in the fundamentalist–modernist dispute, and not much influenced by those who did, they harbor no bitterness and see no reason not to consider the possibility of relating to mainline Protestants as equals—sisters and brothers in Christ. This willingness of left evangelicals to engage in dialogue, fellowship, and joint action with Christians of other persuasions has been apparent for several years. Likewise, some Protestant liberals have initiated conversations with *them*. Left evangelicals have been courted by the NCC and the WCC, mainline Protestant church bureaucrats, major ecumenical and denominational campus ministry organizations, and a number of prominent liberal theological seminaries.

In October 1974 the Unit Committee of the NCC's Division of Church and Society, led by Dean M. Kelley, drafted and approved a positive response to the evangelicals' highly confessional Chicago Declaration. "Moved by the Holy Spirit," the committee declared, "to express a deep feeling of kinship with that statement and with our fellow Christians who issued it," its members responded to each article, themselves confessing that if evangelicals were guilty of neglecting the *social* aspects of the Gospel, they, as liberals (identified as such), had been just as guilty of neglecting the *personal* (or spiritual) aspects:

> We acknowledge that God requires love. But we have not always shown love to those who have disagreed with us on the need to transform the structures of society. We have been too often inclined to criticize or ignore those who have tended to emphasize the personal rather than the structural. . . . We acknowledge that we have not sufficiently shown . . . [the] determination to be rooted in Christ's Gospel. . . . We affirm that God abounds in mercy and that he forgives all who repent and turn from their sins. Se we seek a Christian discipleship that is no longer shy or diffident about proclaiming the complete Gospel of Christ, with both its personal and its social implications.

This moving statement was followed in 1975 by a meeting of NCC top-echelon executives and prominent spokespersons of the evangelical left who had been associated with the Chicago Declaration.

Evangelicals and charismatics were represented at the Fifth General Assembly of the WCC (Nairobi, 1975); few of them, however, were voting delegates appointed by their churches. Among left North American evangelicals attending the assembly were David Hubbard and Mennonite theologian John H. Yoder as advisers; W. Stanley Mooneyham, representing World Vision International; David "Mr. Pentecost" du Plessis as a guest; and Ronald J. Sider of Evangelicals for Social Action and Jim Wallis, editor of *Sojourners* (both of whom felt more kinship with radical Third World participants than with the predominantly left-liberal WCC staff members and denominational delegates). Evangelicals at Nairobi were influential in drafting the report "Confessing Christ Today," adopted unanimously by the assembly. That long report, incidentally, is probably the best statement on holistic evangelism produced by any major ecumenical gathering in recent years. It declares:

> We *deplore* cheap conversions, without consequences. We *deplore* a superficial gospel-preaching, an empty gospel without a call into personal and communal discipleship. . . . We *deplore* conversions without witness to Christ. There are millions who have never heard the good news. We *confess* that we are often ashamed of the gospel. We find it more comfortable to remain in our own Christian circles than to witness in the world. . . . In confessing Christ and in being converted to his Lordship, we experience the freedom of the Holy Spirit and express the ultimate hope for the world.[4]

In July 1975 a dozen left evangelicals and a like number of members of the United Methodist Board of Church and Society held a meeting to discuss the possibility of generating deeper biblical roots to sustain the church's social witness in the apathetic 70s. During 1975–1977 the United Church of Christ, through its Board for Homeland Ministries (traditionally viewed as almost totally secular in its orientation), co-sponsored with invited statewide and regional jurisdictions (conferences) of the UCC eleven open consultations for clergy in key areas of the country to introduce UCC pastors to prominent left evangelical leaders. Although attendance was very good at most of the meetings, and response excellent (especially after the rise of Jimmy Carter), a number of conferences, through their conference ministers (i.e., "bishops"), refused to co-host this kind of gathering, feeling threatened and intimidated by evangelicals—still the victims of outdated stereotypes. The project was indeed successful as a bridge-building effort, the first of its kind initiated and sponsored by a major mainline denomination in the United States since the fundamentalist–modernist controversy (see the special issue of the UCC's magazine, *New Conversations,* Winter–Spring 1976, on "the new evangelicals").

In 1975–1976 The Danforth Foundation and the Lilly Endowment, through Fuller Seminary, funded two national consultations (chaired by Robert Rankin, vice president of Danforth, and David Hubbard) on dialogue with evangelicals in campus ministry, with representatives of just about all the major Protestant, Roman Catholic, and distinctively evangelical campus ministry organizations in the United States (including Campus Crusade for Christ and Inter-Varsity Christian Fellowship). The idea for these explorations came originally from a report to The Danforth Foundation by Robert McAfee Brown of Union Seminary, lamenting the fact that evangelical campus ministries now had all the students who once flooded the denominational and ecumenical campus ministries in the 50s and the activitist 60s. In 1977 there were several regional spinoffs of these consultations, also by invitation, resulting in the potentiality of a new ecumenical student movement in the United States—to be led by IVCF, perhaps, with the aid of evangelically sympathetic campus ministers representing the Lutheran campus ministries, United Ministries in Higher Education (the ecumenical conglomerate of old denominational campus ministry foundations), and even the Roman Catholic campus ministries. Such a movement, still only a remote possibility, would integrate in campus and community ministry evangelism, discipleship, and social action.

Liberal Protestant theological seminaries have also become interested in the evangelical renaissance, especially in its left wing. They have for the first time begun to offer special courses on the belief and work of evangelicals, and a few of them have devoted a whole issue of their in-house scholarly journals to the topic (*explor,* Fall 1976, of United Methodist Garrett–Evangelical Theological Seminary in Evanston, Illinois, and the famous *Union Seminary Quarterly Review,* Winter 1977, for example). Some eminent faculty members at these institutions are themselves coming out as evangelicals, including Old Testament scholar Davie Napier of Pacific School of Religion in Berkeley, California, and Harvey Cox of Harvard Divinity School, who was himself an officer of the Inter-Varsity chapter at the University of Pennsylvania when he was an undergraduate there.[5]

In January 1975 a number of leading Protestant religious thinkers usually identified as liberals joined with Roman Catholics and two Neo-Reformed left evangelicals (Lewis B. Smedes, and Richard Mouw of Calvin College in Grand Rapids) to draft the Hartford Appeal for Theological Affirmation, repudiating thirteen modern "heresies" that they felt had weakened the life of American churches in the twentieth century. The signers of this declaration included William Sloane Coffin, Jr., former chaplain of Yale University, now senior minister of Riverside Church in New York City; sociologist Peter L. Berger; activist Lutheran pastor and senior editor of *Worldview* magazine Richard J. Neuhaus; and Episcopal Bishop of California E. Kilmer Myers. In it, they condemned (among other things) the use of religious language to refer merely to human experience; the understanding of Jesus as a good model of humanity alone; salvation as just the realization of one's potential in this world; sin as failure to realize potential; worship as a way to promote individual self-realization and human community alone; the immanence (rather than transcendence) of God; the notion that "struggle for a better humanity will bring about the Kingdom of God"; the feeling that this life is all there is; and the widespread conviction among theological liberals of recent years that "the world must set the agenda for the church," rather than vice versa.[6] These "heresies," obviously, have indeed been the motivating functional convictions of much of modern theological liberalism as commonly understood, reflected more in ecclesiastical bureaucracies and seminaries than in the local church, however.

It is interesting to note at this point that some mainline Protestant biblical scholars and theologians are now becoming disenchanted with the same literary-historial-critical method of biblical studies that left evangelicals are just beginning to adopt. Academicians of religion like Hans Frei, Brevard Childs, and Paul Holmer of Yale University, and Walter Wink of Auburn Theological Seminary (affiliated with Union), are saying that this kind of biblical criticism (like the Hartford heresies) has sapped the life of the contemporary church, and they are proposing new methods of studying Scripture in its place. In 1976 iconoclast John A. T. Robinson, the eminent British New Testament scholar and author of *Honest to God* the bestselling repudiation of orthodox Christianity, hit the theological community with another bombshell. This one, however, aligns him with some of the most conservative New Testament scholars living today. In *Redating the New Testament,* Robinson takes on some of the sacrosanct conclusions of liberal biblical scholarship that affirm a late authorship for many of the books of the New Testament, and questions the traditional critical views concerning who was responsible for the writings. He insists that *all* the books were written prior to A.D. 70, that Paul wrote *all* the letters attributed to him, and that the Apostle John did indeed write the Fourth Gospel, which, he feels, was in its first draft no later than A.D. 55.

If Protestant liberals are moving toward the right theologically and biblically, they have also recently rediscovered prayer, Bible study (at the personal and corporate levels), spirituality more generally, and evangelism (which no longer means for them social action or church membership recruitment alone). In March 1976 the NCC's Governing Board adopted, almost unanimously, a powerful policy statment on evangelism (formulated largely by Al Krass, co-editor of *The Other Side*). Motivated on the one hand by the continuing decline in membership of its constituent denominations and on the other by the rapid growth of distinctively evangelical and pentecostal denominations, the NCC here confesses the present reluctance of many of its constituents ''to name the Name of Jesus as Lord and Savior.'' Defining the church's evangelistic mandate, the statement concludes by saying:

> The task of evangelism today is calling people to repentance, to faith in Jesus Christ, to study God's word, to continue steadfast in prayer, and to bearing witness to Him. This is a primary function of the church in its congregational,

denominational and ecumenical manifestations. . . . Now, after the journey of the past twenty-five years [the NCC's history], we can call upon people to confess the Name of Jesus Christ and bear witness to that Name in their lives with a fuller understanding of Christian discipleship and a deeper commitment to share the Good News we have found.

This NCC policy statement on evangelism was preceded by a new effort among mainline Protestant denominations (and the Roman Catholic Church as well) to reemphasize evangelism as the call to personal faith in Christ, discipleship, and church membership recruitment (the most important aspect of evangelism for many church bureaucrats whose jobs have been threatened by the membership decline and the resulting decline in support for denominational staff and programs). A front-page article in the April 10, 1977 issue of The New York Times ("Protestant Churches Are Reviving Evangelism in Membership Drive") highlighted the new evangelistic efforts of the Lutheran Church in America, the American Baptist Churches in the U.S.A., The United Presbyterian Church in the U.S.A., The Episcopal Church, The United Methodist Church, and the Christian Church (Disciples of Christ). Equally important here, but not mentioned in the article, have been programs in evangelism designed by the United Church of Christ. The fact that mainline denominations and the NCC and WCC have rediscovered evangelism officially, however, hides the problem that many of their leaders know neither what evangelism really *is* nor what to do with it. Many denominational programs have been put together to train church members in evangelism. They assume that those people are ready and willing to do evangelism but fail to recognize the sad fact that to *do* evangelism, one first has to *be* evangelized (converted) to begin with. Liberal Protestant churches themselves must be evangelized before their members will wholeheartedly evangelize others. *Evangelicals* can do evangelism because they have had an experience of God that they feel they *must* share with others—so powerful an experience that the zeal to witness comes almost naturally. Liberals, if they do not have a describable faith, simply cannot share it with others, despite the finest training programs designed by their denominational bureaucrats.

Obviously, Protestant liberals and evangelicals are moving closer together, aided, as we have noted previously, by the increasing popularity among both groupings of relational theology and the charismatic renewal movement. Official declarations and pronouncements by church bodies, denominational, ecumenical, or evangelical, no longer mean very much by themselves, however—if they ever did in the past. Neither do consultations of academics and the avant-garde elites who "represent" denominations, churches, and parachurch organizations. Nevertheless, they are significant indications, in this case, at least, that the waters of change are rippling. The tidal wave of true ecumenism, however, is yet to come.

Part IV

EVANGELICALS FOR SOCIAL
ACTION AND BEYOND

11

A Statement of Faith
and Works

According to The Gallup Poll, born-again Christians accounted for one third of the American electorate in 1976. (This number included a high percentage of black evangelicals, who most often vote Democratic.) By September of that year, they favored Jimmy Carter for president over Gerald Ford by a wide 58–33 percent margin, despite the fact that white evangelicals in general tend to be more conservative (and more Republican) than the electorate as a whole.[1] Americans United for Separation of Church and State reported that 40 percent of the broad evangelical camp voted for Carter in 1976—twice the number who voted for Hubert Humphrey in 1968 and George McGovern in 1972. Statistics also show that Carter carried 15 of 17 of the heaviest evangelical (albeit largely southern) states in the election.[2]

Jimmy Carter attracted evangelical support, despite his liberal politics, because of his unabashed and believable verbal born-again witness. For the first time in recent history evangelicals could refer to a presidential candidate as a brother in Christ (''Brother Carter'')—a designation reserved by them for born-again believers alone. At his inauguration, which in some ways resembled a sophisticated revival meeting, Carter appealed convincingly to the ideals of America's past (justice, mercy, righteousness, respect, equality, and the need for faith), concepts at the heart of the evangelical faith, even if evangelicals themselves have not always lived up to them. In addition, Carter is different from all his predecessors since Woodrow Wilson, at least, in that his faith in Christ lies at the very center of his life. Furthermore, he was a believer *before* he got into politics. Since the inauguration Carter's regular attendance at Washington, D.C.'s First Baptist Church, his willingness to teach the adult Sunday school class there on occasion, and the high tribute he pays to his sister, Ruth Carter Stapleton, the charismatic faith-healing evangelist, also have pleased most evangelicals. It is not impossible, therefore, that Jimmy Carter may prove to be the catalyst in turning even center and right evangelicals—gradually, to be sure—toward the political left.

We have already noted the leftward trend of younger evangelicals during the past several years, announced publicly by about 50 of their leading spokespersons in the Chicago Declaration of November 1973, which acknowledged that

> God requires justice. But we have not proclaimed or demonstrated his justice to an unjust American society. Although the Lord calls us to defend the social and economic rights of the poor and the oppressed, we have mostly remained silent. . . .
>
> *We must attack* the materialism of our culture and the maldistribution of the nation's wealth and services. We recognize that as a nation we play a crucial role in the imbalance and injustice of international trade and development.
>
> . . . we must challenge the misplaced trust of the nation in economic and military might—a proud trust that promotes a national pathology of war and violence which victimizes our neighbors at home and abroad.

Such words on politics and economics, and an equally strong condemnation of racism and sexism, were shockingly radical at the time for evangelicals whose recent forebears and present kindred regularly have taken the conservative Republican stance on almost every political, economic, and social issue.

Out of the Thanksgiving workshop that produced the Chicago Declaration was born a new organization called Evangelicals for Social Action (ESA), which has included the original declaration signers and a number of other prominent evangelical sympathizers. Follow-up workshops put together to implement the declaration were held in 1974–1976, but little was actually accomplished at these gatherings; it now seems that ESA as a national organization has probably outlived its usefulness, though some other national organization may yet arise to provide a measure of identity and institutional structure to the growing movement of socially concerned left evangelicals.

Ovbiously, much has happened to the evangelical left since 1973. The trend leftward among younger evangelicals has continued unabated, but it has begun to move in several directions as a number of subgroups of left evangelicals have emerged to work out the implications of the Gospel for politics and lifestyle in various different ways.

RADICAL EVANGELICALS: BEYOND THE JESUS MOVEMENT TO POLITICAL AND SOCIAL ACTIVISM

The radical evangelicals stand at the far left of the evangelical left as a whole and are currently the most visible of its subgroups. Many of these Christians were converted in or had a ministry within the Jesus movement of the late 60s and early 70s, where they experienced first-hand communal living and simple, nonmaterialistic styles of life that were very different from the upper-middle-class secular or religious homes in which most of them had been raised. A few radical evangelical leaders had, as students, been active in the civil rights and antiwar struggles of that same period, and even the New Left, where they were exposed to Marxism and the Marxist critique of capitalism. In general, the radical evangelicals have tried to keep the faith as they experienced it in the Jesus movement (and the best traditions of their parent churches), integrating it with the social and political activism they had learned.

The word *radical* (from the Latin *rādix*, root) appears frequently in their writings, and refers to the "radical implications of the biblical message." Its usage among radical evangelicals goes back to two books written by leaders of the Church of the Brethren, Arthur G. Gish's *The New Left and Christian Radicalism,* and Dale Brown's *The Christian Revolutionary*. Both of these authors sought to combine the pacifist, communitarian, simple (and agrarian, really) lifestyle, and low church, "Christ against culture," sixteenth-century Anabaptist (Radical Reformation) heritage of their church, which they share with the Mennonites, with the political and social activism in which they had been involved. Their works have been extremely influential in the development of the radical evangelicals, who use the *radical* designation primarily in either of two ways. First, as Brown suggests (p. 13), it refers to "that which is related to the root, that which is original, fundamental, and inherent" (i.e., first-century Christianity). The second use is put forward by Brown (p. 14) as a "fundamental departure from or challenge to the status quo," exemplified by capitalist America, whose economic and political system (governed by "the principalities and powers," the evil structure of society) is seen as being in essential opposition to Jesus' message and mission.

For radical evangelicals—ideally—there can be no compromise with the established political system which, whatever it happens to be, inevitably becomes corrupt. Gish (p. 30) distinguishes between the radical and liberal stance in viewing politics: "The liberal's norm for action is the system itself or at least what seems possible within the system. . . . The radical rejects the very legitimacy of the establishment and doubts that meaningful change can be brought about through existing structures." Christian responsibility, then, rests in the formation of alternative communities for living and worship that model for the wider society a simple lifestyle, genuine concern and care for the poor and outcast, first-priority commitment to one another as sisters and brothers in Christ, and a prophetic critique of the capitalist system and the institutional church (conservative *and* liberal), which mirrors that system and its values. Many radical evangelicals do not vote or participate in political structures at all. Some, however, work within the establishment as "guerillas" in order to undermine it, but not to bring about change through it. Still others engage in nonviolent protest demonstrations, or do enter electoral politics, but only as a tool by which to educate the public and the church as to the true, evil nature of the system under which we live. Such action, they feel, does not involve compromise, because it does not include operating on the basis of establishment values.[3]

More recently the radical evangelicals have also come under the influence of the brilliant Mennonite theologian, John H. Yoder, whose pivotal work, *The Politics of Jesus,* epitomizes in biblical exegesis and theology the best of the Anabaptist vision, interpreted in the context of modern life. Also highly influential on radical evangelicals has been the eminent French sociologist, author, and lay theologian, Jacques Ellul, whose many books express profoundly his wholesale indictment of existing systems of government, politics, and culture (and their solutions to present problems) as un-Christian. (The June 1977 issue of *Sojourners* is dedicated to Ellul's thought.) Another major influence on radical evangelical theology has been the works of William Stringfellow, the radical Episcopal lay theologian, lawyer, author, and activist, who defended the late Bishop James Pike against heresy charges leveled by leaders of The Episcopal Church, and Daniel and Philip Berrigan, the radical Catholic priests, in their trials for civil disobedience and conspiracy emanating from allegations brought against them by the United States government during the Vietnam War. It was Stringfellow, finally, who brought the witness of the Berrigans (and the Catholic left more generally) to the attention of radical evangelicals. Within the Catholic left, Dorothy Day and the Catholic Worker movement have also profoundly influenced the radical evangelicals. Day (featured in the December 1976 issue of *Sojourners*) has, since the 30s, operated her Catholic Workers' houses of hospitality in major urban ghettos, bringing food, shelter, friendship, and unconditional acceptance to the homeless and oppressed men and women of skid row. By almost any standard, she is a modern-day saint, once abused as a communist and a feminist, but now dearly loved by some of the same people who looked down upon her in the past.

People's Christian Coalition and Sojourners

Three distinctive communities—each with its own journal—function as the most prominent collective expressions of the radical wing of the evangelical left. The first and most famous of the three is the People's Christian Coalition in Washington, D.C. Located now in one of the city's ghettos, the coalition publishes *Sojourners* (formerly the *Post-American*), a monthly magazine edited by Jim Wallis. Founded in 1971 by a group of students at Trinity Evangelical Divinity School and their friends, the People's Christian Coalition moved first from Deerfield, Illinois, to Chicago, and then in 1975 to Washington. Wallis himself, at 29, is a charismatic, forceful leader who was nurtured in a Plymouth Brethren assembly and graduated from Michigan State University, where he had become involved in the New Left. Having dropped out of Trinity (the radicals did not fare well there), Wallis has since then worked full time on his magazine, and is the author of *Agenda for Biblical People,* the radical evangelicals' foremost manifesto. *Sojourners* (deriving its name from the biblical metaphor for the people of God who live in the world as "strangers, pilgrims, aliens") is currently the "chic" religious publicaticn in the United States, taking over from *Christianity and Crisis* (founded in New York City by Reinhold Niebuhr and John C. Bennett during World War II), and read avidly not only by left evangelicals but also by left-liberal church bureaucrats and seminary professors. Its investigative reporting, moreover, is a thorn in the side for conservative evangelicals and its contributing editors include prominent left evangelicals like Lucille Sider Dayton (whose husband Donald has been book review editor); Samuel Escobar; Senator Mark Hatfield (whose former executive assistant, Wes Michaelson, is managing editor); Bill Pannell; Clark Pinnock; Anglican charismatic leader Graham Pulkingham (who was formerly rector of Houston's Church of the Redeemer); British Anglican priest John R. W. Stott (the Inter-Varsity hero); William Stringfellow; and John H. Yoder.

It should be noted at this point that not all the people associated with *Sojourners* are members of the residential coalition or share all of its values. The community itself has undergone many ups and downs and a great turnover in membership since its inception, and it is run by Wallis and a few other ''elders.''

Sojourners itself—which really *is* Jim Wallis—focuses especially upon capitalist exploitation in the United States and abroad, and upon violence, racism, sexism, militarism, materialism, and the foibles of both conservative and liberal Christendom and their equal alignment with the dominant American culture. More than other publications of the evangelical left, it has been the most open to using New Left and Marxist categories (including arguments raised by liberation theology) as part of its critique, despite its deep commitment to nonviolence in principle. As editor of *Sojourners,* Wallis has become the most eminent young evangelical leader.

The Other Side

The second prominent radical evangelical community is located in a relatively middle-class section of Philadelphia and publishes *The Other Side,* a bimonthly magazine, less doctrinaire (and less Anabaptist) and a bit more conservative than *Sojourners* (though its June 1976 issue did express basic agreement with the Jewett biblical hermeneutic). The community itself is not communal in nature. Families and singles simply live nearby in the neighborhood, not all together in a few big houses like the

People's Christian Coalition. *The Other Side* was founded in 1965 as *Freedom Now* by Fred Alexander to raise issues of racial injustice among evangelical and fundamentalist Christians. It is now co-edited by John F. Alexander, the founder's son, a brilliant but humble graduate of Oxford University and Trinity Evangelical Divinity School who once taught philosophy at Wheaton College; Mark Olson, a long-time associate of the magazine; and Al Krass, a former United Church of Christ missionary to Ghana and evangelism consultant to the UCC's Board for World Ministries. Recently the community, under the leadership of Judy Alexander, created two new ministries—Jubilee Crafts and Jubilee Fund (named after the Old Testament jubilee year). Jubilee Crafts buys and imports fine handcrafted products from Third World workers, sells them in the United States at reasonable prices, and returns all profits to the workers themselves (represented by worker-owned Christian cooperatives). Jubilee Fund supports education, housing, and development projects initiated by indigenous people in very poor parts of the world, which focus on development, social change, and justice, not simply relief in time of disaster or otherwise.

Berkeley Christian Coalition and Rādix

The third notable radical evangelical community was begun in 1969 in Berkeley, California, as the Christian World Liberation Front (CWLF)—a "front" for Campus Crusade for Christ to evangelize radical and countercultural students and street people by adopting their dress, language, and basic lifestyles, but not their politics. Unfortunately for Crusade, however, CWLF was itself radicalized politically in the process of its ministry, and now fits in well with the Berkeley left more generally.[4]

After a major split in 1975, CWLF changed its name and, later, also the name of its newspaper to the Berkeley Christian Coalition (BCC). *Right On* became *Rādix* (now a bimonthly). The BCC functions on a very democratic basis and currently has several different ministries, including Dwight House, a "crash pad" for transients coming to Berkeley; Abrigo Ranch in Tres Pinos, built to support long-term efforts to rehabilitate alienated people living in Berkeley and elsewhere; a Spiritual Counterfeits Project (not unlike Walter R. Martin's); a house church, based on low-church principles (but otherwise similar to Catholic models of the

6os); The Crucible, a program of theological education for laity; a campus ministry, led by former Campus Crusade staffer Gary Gates; and *Rādix,* of course.

Rādix is edited by Sharon Gallagher. Like *The Other Side,* The BCC's newspaper is less doctrinaire than *Sojourners,* and it regularly discusses current films and the arts in general. Gallagher, a Westmont College graduate, now in her late 2os, is also a leader in the evangelical feminist movement. Like Wallis, she was raised in a Plymouth Brethren home.

Each of these three radical evangelical communities has less than 100 active members and is made up predominantly of young, white, well-educated singles from upper-middle-class evangelical backgrounds, though all of them are seeking to include more minorities (blacks, in particular), married couples with children, and older people. And though they won't admit it, all three communities are gradually moving toward an espousal of some form of Christian socialism, tinged with Marxism.

THE NEW CALVINISTS

The Neo-Reformed evangelicals stand to the liberal right of the radical evangelicals both in politics and in lifestyle. They are Calvinists of the first order but are not to be confused with leaders of the evangelical establishment whose Calvinism is derived from the Reformed scholasticism of the Old Princeton school of theology. Neo-Reformed evangelicals have been deeply influenced by the neo-orthodoxy of Barth (many of them are members of the Karl Barth Society), Bonhoeffer, Brunner, and Reinhold Niebuhr. They tend to be Christian realists in the tradition of Niebuhr, who argued that the *social* expression of Christian love is justice. Society, permeated by human sin, simply cannot live by pure ideals; thus it must accept the limited possibilities given by political actualities (for instance, war may be an evil, but sometimes it is a necessary evil). Nevertheless, Niebuhr did see the relevance of an impossible ethical ideal (i.e., Christian love), since it does inspire individuals to strive for maximum social justice. Neo-Reformed evangelicals are generally content to live a middle-class lifestyle (many of them are comfortable suburbanites), and they are not pacifists.

In addition to neo-orthodoxy, two other sources have shaped the thinking of Neo-Reformed evangelicals: First, a serious commitment to seeking justice and righteousness, especially as proclaimed by the Old

Testament prophets and by the Jesus of the Synoptic Gospels; second, a Reformed Calvinist orthodoxy rooted in the thought of a number of Dutch theologians and philosophers, such as G. C. Berkouwer and the late Herman Dooyeweerd, both of the Free University of Amsterdam.

Unlike the radical evangelicals, the Neo-Reformed evangelicals understand Christian discipleship to require responsible participation in the political process for the greater realization of justice and righteousness in the world. Among their most prominent leaders, Richard Mouw, a framer of both the Chicago Declaration and the Hartford Appeal, argues in *Politics and the Biblical Drama* that involvement in the structures and institutions of the present age is not a mere "holding action." Rather, it is a legitimate means of preparation for life in the Kingdom of God, which is yet to come in its fullness. Contrary to Yoder and Wallis, Mouw insists that God will allow our present individual political activities to count as preparatory signs of his coming Kingdom. Paul B. Henry, also of Calvin College, was chairperson of the Kent County (Grand Rapids) Republican Party (Gerald Ford's political base), and has been described by his father, Carl F. H. Henry, as a "liberal conservative."[5] In *Politics for Evangelicals* he pleads for evangelical political participation and chastises traditional evangelicals for their indifference to politics, which he sees as based upon their characteristic gnostic denial of the immediacy and reality of the Kingdom in the world. Henry also tends to treat political engagement as a test of orthodoxy. Stephen Monsma, formerly of Calvin College as well, was recently elected a Democratic representative to the Michigan House. More liberal than Henry, Monsma, in *The Unraveling of America,* condemns evangelical neglect of political structures as a whole.

A number of Neo-Reformed evangelicals are or have been associated with Calvin College (Christian Reformed Church). Many among them, however, are United Presbyterians and Baptists, and some of them (Lewis B. Smedes, James Daane, Jack Rogers, and Paul K. Jewett, for example) teach at Fuller Seminary. Politically, the Neo-Reformed evangelicals range from moderate Republicans (Henry supported Ford in 1976 but criticized his poor record on environmental issues and slowness in advancing civil rights concerns) to liberal Democrats. Political leaders among them include Republican Congressman from Illinois John B. Anderson, author of *Vision and Betrayal in America,* and Republican Senator Mark Hatfield of Oregon, a Baptist and original signer of the

Chicago Declaration, whose book, *Between a Rock and a Hard Place,* and association with *Sojourners* suggests further movement toward the radical left. Then, of course, there is Jimmy Carter, a typically Baptist Calvinist in his view of the inherent sinfulness of human nature, even "in Christ" (reflected vividly in his November 1976 *Playboy* interview), whose high regard for Reinhold Niebuhr is well known.

Neo-Reformed evangelical views are presented most regularly in books published by Eerdmans and in *The Reformed Journal* (Grand Rapids), whose managing editor is Marlin Van Elderen. This monthly magazine is now one of the most sophisticated semischolarly theological publications in the United States. It consistently grapples with current social issues (recently, it took a stand *against* the proposed Right to Life amendment to the Constitution and has expressed much disdain for the total inerrancy position held by Lindsell and Schaeffer). Another prominent Neo-Reformed evangelical monthly, *Vanguard,* which has been edited by Bonnie Greene, is published by the Institute for Christian Studies in Toronto, an independent graduate faculty of scholars (including C. T. McIntire, son of the separatist fundamentalist radio preacher Carl McIntire). *Vanguard* is committed to examining, from a strongly traditional yet avant-garde Reformed stance, "the implications of a Christian view of human nature, the creation, evil and redemption, culture and society, knowledge, justice, stewardship, and aesthetic engagement."

Neo-Reformed evangelicals constitute what is perhaps the largest and most literate subgroup of the evangelical left. Their stance may well become dominant among the evangelical intelligensia as a whole, and among evangelical political leaders generally.

THE NEW WESLEYANS

John Wesley wrote an interesting definition of "the character of a Methodist," recently abridged, paraphrased, and put into modern-day English by Good News. In this work the founder of Methodism answers the question, "What are the distinguishing marks of a Methodist?" saying, in part:

> The distinguishing marks of a Methodist are not his opinions of any sort . . . his accepting this or that scheme of religion . . . his embracing any particular

set of notions . . . or mouthing the judgements of one man or another. All these are quite wide of the point. . . .

Nor is a Methodist identified because he bases his religion on any particular *part* of God's truth. By "salvation," the Methodist means holiness of heart and life. . . .

A Methodist is a person who has the love of God in his heart. . . .

Inscribed indelibly on the Methodist's heart is the truth that "he who loves God loves his brother also." This means that the Methodist cares about his neighbor as much as the Methodist cares about himself!

His heart is full of love—for everyone. . . . Even those who hate the Methodist receive love in return. For like Jesus, the Methodist loves his enemies. And the Methodist loves God's enemies, the evil and the unthankful.

. . . God has cleansed the Methodist's heart, washing away all urge for revenge . . . all envy . . . all wrath . . . all desire for harming another person. Every unkind inclination is gone . . . every evil lust and desire too. Pride has been purged out of the Methodist mind and heart. Gone also is haughtiness which always causes friction between people. . . .

Not only does the Methodist AIM at complete dedication to God, he achieves this! [i.e., entire sanctification, or holiness]

. . . He cannot devote himself to selfish indulgence. The Methodist can no more be preoccupied with making money than he could swallow red hot embers! . . .

The Christian thinks, speaks, and lives according to the pattern set by Jesus. And his soul is renewed in righteousness and holiness, after God's own image. . . . And so I beg you, let all true Christians remain united; let us not be divided among ourselves. Is your heart right as my heart is with yours? I ask no further question; give me your hand. For the sake of mere opinions or terms, let us not destroy the work of God.

Do you love God? This is enough. I give you the right hand of fellowship.[6]

Sharing a parallel vision with the Calvinist Neo-Reformed evangelicals, the Arminian Neo-Wesleyan evangelicals—also to the liberal right of the radical evangelicals in lifestyle and politics—emphasize, like Wesley himself (more so than the Neo-Reformed evangelicals), right practice over orthodox doctrine, and stress Wesley's "social holiness" and genuine ecumenicity. Many of them are United Methodists; members of the smaller holiness denominations like The Salvation Army, The Wesleyan Church, the Free Methodist Church of North America, and the Church of God (Anderson, Indiana); or members of pentecostal denominations like the Pentecostal Holiness Church and the International Church of the Foursquare Gospel (founded by Aimee Semple McPherson).

Professor and philosopher Merold Westphal of Hope College, Holland, Michigan, argues for a hermeneutic that allows the radical power of the biblical message to be immediately present. Nevertheless, he insists, in an unpublished paper, "the fear of the Lord, not hermeneutical reflection, is the beginning of wisdom. Or, to paraphrase Marx, the theologians have only interpreted the Bible differently—the task is to obey." Against the Anabaptist radical evangelicals, Westphal calls for a biblically realistic political involvement, declaring that "citizenship requires imitating the Kingdom in a context which will not finally belong to it."

Other prominent leaders of the Neo-Wesleyan subgroup of the evangelical left include Donald W. Dayton; Howard K. Snyder, executive director of Light and Life Men International (Free Methodist) and author of *The Problem of Wineskins: Church Structure in a Technological Age;* Stephen C. Mott of Gordon-Conwell Theological Seminary; and H. Vinson Synan, general secretary of the Pentecostal Holiness Church, and author of *The Holiness-Pentecostal Movement in the United States.*

THE NEW BLACKS

To most blacks the word *evangelical* has little historical relevance; *Bible believing* is the more widely used descriptive term. Because until recent times blacks rarely used the word *evangelical* to distinguish themselves from other confessing Christians, it has been erroneously assumed that there is very little true evangelical Christianity within the black church as a whole. Blacks trained in white Bible schools, colleges, and seminaries were confronted with this defective analysis of the black church. It was often argued in those institutions, for instance, that evangelical orthodoxy is incompatible with the free expression of emotion—in preaching, singing, and worship more generally—in the less status-oriented black churches. Thus black evangelical leaders became ashamed of their religious tradition, and tried to impose white standards and values on a people who had been historical victims of those same values and standards. In fact, black evangelicalism, with the exception of black pentecostalism, perhaps, is a distinctively middle-class phenomenon, and has much more in common with its white counterpart than with the black mainstream denominations that were really responsible for the survival of black people and black culture in the United States.

Bible believers are to be found in all the major black mainstream denominations, such as the National Baptist Convention U.S.A., Inc.; the National Baptist Convention of America; the Progressive National Baptist Convention, Inc.; the African Methodist Episcopal Church; the African Methodist Episcopal Zion Church; and the Christian Methodist Episcopal Church—which together encompass a very large amount of evangelical sentiment among their more than eleven million members (eight million Baptists alone). Biblical believers are also found among the one million blacks who often joined white denominations as a result of upward social mobility. They comprise the whole membership of distinctively evangelical and fundamentalist churches and denominations of black Christianity like the Brethren Assemblies (offshoots of the Plymouth Brethren) and independent or fundamentalist Baptist churches, in addition to the black holiness and pentecostal denominations, the largest of which is the (pentecostal) Church of God in Christ.[7]

Unlike their white counterparts, the new black evangelicals do not look with contempt on the recent history of their inherited religious tradition. They stress the fact that black evangelicals *and* fundamentalists have never separated evangelism from social concern the way white theological conservatives have. The new black evangelicals focus their efforts on the struggle against racism, strengthening black identity and traditional black culture, and building up the larger black community. Mainly Democrats and Baptists (with an increasing number of pentecostals among them), they are committed church people who believe strongly in working to transform existing ecclesiastical and political structures. Most of them disagree with the radical evangelicals' emphasis on creating alternative communities rather than working within the system. In other words, why should blacks, who are finally beginning to "make it" in the wider society, go back to poverty (albeit voluntary poverty) and the urban ghettos where many of the radicals now live? Finally, like other black Christians, new black evangelicals have gained inspiration from reading the theological works on black liberation by Union Seminary Professor James Cone.[8]

Leading new black evangelical fellowship associations and ministries include the National Black Evangelical Association (NBEA), founded in Los Angeles in 1963, when it appeared that the predominantly white

NAE was not meeting the needs of blacks. (It is interesting to note that the program guide of the NBEA's 1977 annual convention in San Francisco contained the black national anthem, "Lift Every Voice and Sing," and tributes to famous black Americans including Marxists W. E. B. DuBois and Angela Davis—the likes of which would never be found in a comparable NAE program guide.) NBEA currently has its headquarters in South Ozone Park, New York.

Voice of Calvary (Mendenhall, Mississippi), headed by John Perkins, author of *Let Justice Roll Down* and *A Quiet Revolution,* has implemented a unique program of social activism and evangelistic outreach. In an area of Mississippi where blacks face some of the worst racial and economic conditions, Perkins and his integrated staff of workers have developed a wide-ranging program of health care, cooperatives, small businesses, housing rehabilitation, education, and counseling, as well as personal evangelism.

Tom Skinner Associates (New York City) is directed by Tom Skinner, the eminent black evangelist who first raised the consciousness of white evangelicals en masse about the evils of racism at Inter-Varsity Christian Fellowship's Urbana '70, saying:

> To a great extent the evangelical church in America supported the status quo. It supported slavery; it supported segregation; it preached against any attempt of the black man to stand on his own two feet. And those who sought to communicate the gospel to black people did it in a way to make sure that they stayed cool. "We will preach the gospel to those folks so they won't riot; we will preach the gospel to them so that we can keep the lid on the garbage pail." And so they were careful to point out such scriptures as, "Obey your masters," "Love your enemy," "Do good to them that hurt you." But no one ever talked about a message which would also speak to the oppressor. [9]

Tom Skinner's organization is growing and now engages in mass evangelistic meetings; a weekly half-hour radio broadcast ("Tom Skinner Speaks"); a literature ministry that features the evangelist's books, including *If Christ Is The Answer, What Are the Questions?,* campus and community ministries to blacks; a music ministry featuring the gospel rock group Soul Liberation II; and a black leadership development program [10].

Prominent new black evangelical leaders, most of whom helped frame the Chicago Declaration, including Skinner; Perkins; Bill Pannell, author of *My Friend the Enemy*; Bill Bentley, Fuller Seminary's first black graduate and former president of the NBEA; Ruth Lewis Bentley, head of minority affairs at the University of Illinois Medical School in Chicago; sociologist Ozzie Edwards of the University of Michigan; Wesley Roberts of Gordon-Conwell Theological Seminary; Wyn Wright Potter, NBEA executive secretary; Ron Potter, associate of *The Other Side;* and Clarence Hilliard, chairperson of the NAE's Evangelical Social Action Commission.

THE NEW CATHOLICS

For another subgroup of the evangelical left, the search for theological roots has turned to rediscovery of the Catholic heritage in the Anglican and Roman Catholic traditions. Among the new Catholic evangelicals (deeply influenced by C. S. Lewis, who was himself an active Anglo-Catholic layman), there has been a self-conscious attempt to relate evangelical Christianity to the ongoing Christian faith. These Christians recognize that the church was not born from the twentieth-century fundamentalist–modernist controversy, nor from eighteenth- and nineteenth-century revivalism, nor from the sixteenth-century Reformation. Rather, its roots go back fifteen centuries earlier.

Robert Webber of Wheaton College articulates the new Catholic evangelical stance by arguing that the revitalization of evangelicalism, in ecclesiology, worship, theology, mission, and spirituality, requires the recovery and reaffirmation of pre-Reformation orthodoxy as expressed especially by the Fathers and the ecumenical councils.[11] Thus the new Catholic evangelicals display a variety of interesting characteristics not usually associated with evangelical Christianity. Priority is placed on worship, the sacraments, liturgy, renewed spirituality, Christian unity, and the *institutional church* as the normal means by which the reconciliation of the world to God is achieved. The church is seen as a transforming, sacramental presence in the world, God's instrument of action. And the modern sociopolitical crisis is viewed as being essentially religious, requiring a fundamentally religious solution with radical implications on both a personal and corporate level.

For the new Catholic evangelicals, the religious nature of the problem and its religious solution are of crucial importance. The problem of culture is viewed by them as being rooted in radical secularization, which represents willful human rebellion against God. The solution will come only through the active presence and grace of God, involving a Christian faith lived fully in the world. To this end these Christians, like their Neo-Reformed, Neo-Wesleyan, and new black evangelical sisters and brothers, believe in working through the established political structures to change them from within—and in the Christ who transforms culture.

The new Catholic evangelicals find the roots of faith in the historic stream of Catholic orthodoxy as much as in the Bible itself. By emphasizing a sacramental view of God's action in history through the institutional church—the visible community of faith—they stand in opposition both to religious sectarianism and to blatant secularism.

In May 1977 a gathering (planned originally by Webber) was called in Chicago to draw up a confessional statement with which the emerging new Catholic evangelicals (most of whom come from fundamentalist or conservative evangelical backgrounds) could identify. Entitled "The Chicago Call: An Appeal to Evangelicals," [12] it is an amazing document for evangelicals to have written—one that the World Council of Churches might look at with high regard—affirming: (1) "historic roots and continuity" (reclaiming the whole historic Christian Tradition); (2) "biblical fidelity"; (3) "creedal identity" (with the ecumenical creeds, the Reformation confessions, and contemporary statements in addition to Scripture); (4) "holistic salvation" (including personal conversion, physical and emotional healing, social justice for "the oppressed and disinherited," and ecological stewardship of the natural world); (5) "sacramental integrity" (almost totally lacking among evangelicals); (6) "spirituality" (including the disciplines of prayer, meditation, silence, fasting, Bible study, and spiritual diaries); (7) "church authority" (needed ecclesiastical discipline); and (8) the first *major* evangelical expression of "church unity":

> We deplore the scandalous isolation and separation of Christians from one another. We believe such division is contrary to Christ's explicit desire for unity among his people and impedes the witness of the church in the world. Evangelicalism is too frequently characterized by an ahistorical, sectarian mentality. We fail to appropriate the catholicity of historic Christianity, as well as the breadth of the biblical revelation. [13]

Among the original signers of "The Chicago Call," besides Webber, are author Thomas Howard of Gordon College, an Episcopal layman, and

Lane T. Dennis, a United Presbyterian minister, associate of *The Other Side,* and author of *A Reason for Hope.* All three are prominent new Catholic evangelical leaders.

These subgroups of the evangelical left are, of course, tentative expressions of emerging differences in politics, lifestyle, and theological emphasis within the evangelical left as a whole. Other subgroups that find their roots elsewhere will, no doubt, also appear, while the existing ones may grow or wane or coalesce in the course of their further development.[14]

MESSIANIC JEWS

At this point, one additional young evangelical movement, which does not really fit into any typology of evangelical Christianity (right, center, or left), needs to be mentioned, since it offers one of the clearest examples of modern Christians going back to their cultural roots. The *Messianic Jews,* as they often term themselves, are trying to reestablish the earliest days of the church, when Christians were accepted as being Jews. Although Messianic Jews hold to orthodox Christian doctrines, they usually shun labels such as *convert* (to Christianity), and even *Christian.* Many of them retain Jewish traditions like Saturday worship, keeping Jewish holidays with feasting and dancing, and the wearing of skullcaps. Some of them call their leaders *rabbis* and their meeting places *synagogues.* Because the established Jewish community feels that these Messianic Jews are really Christian evangelists masquerading as Jews to gain converts (many of whom are young Jews from the very liberal Reformed tradition of Judaism), it is extremely upset by their actions.

The movement itself began in the late 60s with the Jesus movement, and it is estimated that perhaps 10,000–20,000 young U.S. Jews (though not all Messianic Jews are young) have decided to follow Jesus (Yeshua). Some of the movement's subgroups are made up of very zealous charismatics who stress evangelism; others are quieter, and emphasize their Jewishness over witnessing and emotionally oriented worship. Most famous among the Messianic Jewish leaders is Moishe Rosen, who founded Jews for Jesus in 1973 and now leads a staff of 60, with a $2 million annual budget, from his headquarters in San Rafael, California.

Although Jewish authorities hold that a Jew who adopts Christianity or any other religious tradition is an apostate and a grievous sinner (and forgiveness is not central to Judaism), he or she remains technically a Jew, since the Talmud says that "a Jew who sins is still a Jew."[15] Unlike the evangelical left, Messianic Jews do not yet appear to be much interested in politics (except when it concerns Israel). Some of them, moreover, hold an almost fundamentalist theology behind their Jewishness. At the same time, however, their Jewish lifestyle, with its traditional feasting, drinking, and dancing, is not generally acceptable to many evangelicals of the center and right (though evangelicals of all theological stripes do support them). And, like Jesus, they are indeed Jews.

12

Today's Evangelicals,
Tomorrow's Liberals?

Unlike Socrates, evangelicals have always preferred answers over questions. But, in the words of Tom Skinner, if Christ is the answer, what are the questions? In trying to understand the evangelicals today, we are faced with four important questions.

WILL NEW CENTERS OF EVANGELICAL POWER EMERGE?

First, will new centers of evangelical power and conviction emerge to provide identity and leadership for a movement in transition? Until the 70s, the evangelical subculture, born in the early 40s out of fundamentalism, was led by three major organizations that functioned, symbolically at least, to define evangelicalism and give it direction—the National Association of Evangelicals, the Billy Graham Evangelistic Association, and the Evangelical Theological Society. The NAE identified evangelical church life; the Billy Graham Evangelistic Association, evangelism; and the ETS, theology. They provided an identity for evangelicals and set ecclesiastical and ideological boundaries for a movement still relatively homogeneous in character—white, middle-class, male-dominated, Calvinist, revivalistic, and politically conservative.

With the collapse of the establishment evangelical subculture itself and the broadening of evangelical theology, these three organizations, and their "official" mouthpiece, *Christianity Today,* no longer represent, lead, or provide identity for a growing number of evangelicals who affirm the full authority of the Bible, the need for conversion to Christ, and the mandate for evangelism, but do not fit into the traditional evangelical mold—namely, minorities, the poor, feminists, Wesleyans and other Arminians, charismatics, Anabaptists, Catholics, political liberals and radicals, gays, and intellectuals—people who accept biblical criticism, evolution, the scientific method, and broad cultural analysis, while rejecting the cultural taboos and the ethos of modern revivalism. Thus new centers of evangelical conviction and power have indeed begun to emerge to provide direction and leadership for these American Christians.

Among them are the National Black Evangelical Association, Evangelicals for Social Action (and whatever new organization will descend from it), the Evangelical Women's Caucus, the Wesleyan Theological Society, the Society for Pentecostal Studies, Evangelicals Concerned, and a number of prominent evangelical magazines and newspapers like *Sojourners, R adix, The Other Side, The Wittenburg Door, The Reformed Journal, Vanguard, Faith at Work,* and *Catholic Charismatic* (Ramsey, New Jersey). Even the NAE, the Billy Graham Evangelistic Association, and the ETS—still strong—may, ultimately, be forced to modify their present positions and accommodate themselves to a broadening evangelical movement rather than sink into sectarianism and isolationism. A more heterogeneous evangelicalism will require a more diverse network of organizational leadership, and evangelical unity in the future will have to be unity in a great deal of diversity.

WILL EVANGELICALS RENEW THE ECUMENICAL QUEST?

Second, is there a larger ecumenical significance to the fact that evangelicals and Protestant liberals are becoming more like each other? The postfundamentalist evangelical subculture limited its cooperation with other Christians to those who shared and confessed its doctrinal affirmations, specifically the doctrine of total biblical inerrancy (which, of course, was a *particular* affront to Protestant liberals). But the evangelical left (and more conservative evangelicals too), aided by charismatic renewal, relational theology, a rejection of total inerrancy, broad cultural analysis, and a new ecumenical vision, are now moving toward nonevangelicals—Protestants and Catholics—with outstretched arms. At the same time many nonevangelicals themselves, aided by a fresh interest in prayer, personal and corporate Bible study, evangelism, and spirituality, are moving toward the evangelicals. In fact, we may soon see a powerful resurgence of ecumenism among evangelicals that will renew the ecumenical quest popular among Protestant liberals in the early 60s; "We seek a church that is truly Catholic, truly Evangelical, and truly Reformed." This possibility is indicated in "The Chicago Call":

> Therefore we call for a recovery of our full Christian heritage. Throughout the church's history there has existed an evangelical impulse to proclaim the saving, unmerited grace of Christ, and to reform the church according to the Scriptures. The impulse appears in the doctrines of the ecumenical councils, the piety of the early fathers, the Augustinian theology of grace, the zeal of the monastic reformers, the devotion of the practical mystics and the scholarly integrity of the Christian humanists. It flowers in the biblical fidelity of the Protestant Reformers and the ethical earnestness of the Radical Reformation. It continues in the efforts of the Puritans and Pietists to complete and perfect the Reformation. It is reaffirmed in the awakening movements of the eighteenth and nineteenth centuries which joined Lutheran, Reformed, Wesleyan and other evangelicals in an ecumenical effort to renew the church and to extend its mission in the proclamation and social demonstration of the Gospel. It is present at every point in the history of Christianity where the Gospel has come to expression through the operation of the Holy Spirit: in some of the strivings toward renewal in Eastern Orthodoxy and Roman Catholicism and in biblical insights in forms of Protestantism differing from our own. We dare not move beyond the biblical limits of the Gospel; but we cannot be fully evangelical without recognizing our need to learn from other times and movements concerning the whole meaning of that Gospel (p. 1).

Evangelicals must recognize that no matter how convinced they are that they have "the truth," biblically, no one is promised *all* of that truth in this life. We see through a glass, darkly. Others—even Catholics and Protestant liberals—may have much to teach the evangelicals. Furthermore, God is the ultimate judge of all our theologies, and Jesus has commanded us to love everyone, whether liberal, evangelical, or atheist, even our enemies. This should itself provide sufficient grounds for dialogue, fellowship, and joint action among Christians of differing views.

ARE EVANGELICALS REALLY MOVING TO THE THEOLOGICAL LEFT?

Third, and very simply, are evangelicals really becoming liberals? Robert S. Ellwood, Jr. of the School of Religion at the University of Southern California has asked

Is the new evangelicalism . . . really something new *within* evangelicalism, or is [it] the shaky, searching first steps of a reborn liberalism? For while the new evangelicals avoid like the plague any language suggestive of mature "social gospel," "modernist," or "secular theology" liberalism, their theology on basic points like the meaning of Scripture seems to involve some subtle shifts in the direction of the seminal liberalism of Schleiermacher, Maurice, or Bushnell. I wondered if history were not repeating itself rather than doing something new . . . perhaps paralleling the well-known changes in rhetoric and style that evangelical churches like the Methodist underwent several generations ago as their constituencies moved up the education and affluence ladders.[1]

We can add to Ellwood's analysis our previous discussion about the theological similarities between the evangelical left and classical neo-orthodoxy (its biblical and systematic theology) and the kind of neo-liberalism that John C. Bennett represents—in part, the result of the continued upward social mobility of the evangelicals as a whole and their new stress on experiential (e.g., charismatic) and relational theology, not unlike the liberal Friedrich Schleiermacher and the existentialist Soren Kierkegaard.

In the past disgruntled evangelicals readily became liberals in word and deed, because Protestant liberalism and its churches provided a viable, dynamic Christian alternative for intellectuals, doubters, relativists, and clergy and laity who no longer wished to observe the traditional personal moral taboos enforced by evangelicalism at the time. But with the loss of vitality of theological liberalism, unhappy evangelicals no longer see it as an attractive option. Now, however, the evangelical left provides a better option for evangelicals who may still *believe* like evangelicals, but wish to *behave* like liberals. Furthermore, among this group there may be an increasingly large number of people who really *have* moved beyond evangelical belief toward liberalism. In other words, they have rejected the evangelical position intellectually (though they may not admit or even recognize it), but they still have an *emotional* attachment to the movement in which they were converted and nurtured. This unfortunate stance is especially characteristic of a number of graduates of left evangelical seminaries (like Fuller), who were reared in conservative denominations and homes, affiliated with a mainline denomination while in seminary (like The United Presbyterian Church in the U.S.A.), and became pastor or associate pastor of a liberal congregation in that denomination. Thus some evangelicals *are* becoming liberals without saying so. But it is still too early to discern where this current trend will lead.

WILL SUCCESS SPOIL THE EVANGELICALS?

Fourth, and finally, how should we interpret the profound influence of the wider culture on the evangelicals today? The church—including the evangelical church—is a social institution of men and women who live and work in secular society. It therefore reflects, to one degree or another, the concerns and values of the wider culture in which it is situated. In the twentieth century Protestant liberalism has accommodated itself to culture more quickly than evangelicism, which *can* be viewed as a movement 10, 20, 30, or even 100 years behind the times, behind the *Zeitgeist,* or spirit of the age. Clearly, evangelicalism is catching up with that spirit and making up for lost time in the process. Culture is not inherently evil. But in the biblical context, the values of culture must always be put in second place to the values of Jesus. When cultural values take priority over the values of Jesus in the life of a Christian, when a given value of the wider culture claims his or her ultimate loyalty, then it becomes an idol, and must be rejected. In the New Testament *the world* does not signify all of culture, only those aspects of culture that are self-glorifying and rebellious against God.

The evangelical right and center has been affected by one set of values of the wider American culture—upward social mobility, financial success (reflecting the Protestant work ethic), popularity (symbolized by church growth), social respectability (witness the adulation of national celebrities who are converted), and allegiance to the political status quo. Only insofar as center and right evangelicals make an idol out of these values are they being unfaithful to the Gospel. The evangelical left, for the most part, has been influenced by *another* set of values of the wider American culture—education and intellectual respectability, relativism, pluralism, political and cultural liberalism, socialism (traditionally valued by left academics and church bureaucrats), and revolution. By idolizing these values, they, too, will be unfaithful to the Gospel. A conservative evangelical pastor who lives in a $150,000 home, drives a Mercedes Benz 450SL, and presides over a multi-million-dollar church complex—if he or she makes an idol out of that—is not necessarily more unfaithful to the Gospel than a radical evangelical who lives in an urban commune, does not own a car, makes $2000 a year, and presides over a house church, but glorifies his or her simple lifestyle with a smug self-righteousness that puts down more middle-class Christians. The temptation to idolatry is always with us.

The evangelicals—right, center, and left—once a despised minority, are rapidly becoming the respectable (even chic) religious majority, the new religious establishment, in America. Let them beware. Historically, since the time of Constantine, whenever the church has become "established"—too popular, too respectable—corruption and secularism have become rampant within its ranks. Despite their tendencies toward self-righteousness and sectarianism (fundamentalism of the left), their frequent lack of good humor and a doctrine of grace, the radical evangelicals may be pointing the church as a whole in the right direction, because Christianity, at its biblical core, is neither a conservative nor a liberal option. It is downright radical. "Love your enemies." How radical can you get? Christ demands that his followers take up their cross and travel a narrow way that can never be popular. In many ways that demand challenges almost all the values of the wider culture that Christians often take up as a *compromise* because the way of the cross is just too hard.

God leaves us to work out our own salvation with "fear and trembling." Followers of Jesus Christ are to be "in the world but not of it." Some of us may not share all the insights of Edith Black, a young evangelical convert who grew up in a liberal United Church of Christ home, and most of us are on a different spiritual pilgrimage altogether. Nevertheless, I cannot think of a more appropriate way to sum up the highest ideals of the evangelical witness than to share her story, "A Rediscovery of the Christian Faith," from the inaugural issue, Winter 1973, of *Radical Religion* (Berkeley, California) as my conclusion:

A Rediscovery of the Christian Faith

EDITH BLACK

I know God as a deliverer. When I was at Union Theological Seminary I encountered God in the liberation movements of which I was a participant—in the civil rights, anti-war, and student movements and in women's liberation. The God of the Biblical faith was for me the one who heard the cries of the oppressed and who delivered them. I saw the dialectic of judgement and grace being worked out in the midst of social upheaval. I steeped myself in the prophets and developed, by exhaustive reading of Marxist theory, a sharply analytical, prophetic critique of American capitalism. But for me in those exciting march-filled days God was always out there, fighting an oppressor that was out there, an oppressor in the evil structure of society, the principalities and powers. I had little understanding of the oppressor inside the deepest part of each of us.

My deep involvement in the movement enriched me tremendously and in no way do I look back on it with regret. But like so many other dedicated radicals, I quickly burned out. Why? For a long time I didn't understand why, but now I think I know. I initially dropped out because my health broke down, but it wasn't this that kept me out, for had I known a loving, empathetic response to being sick on the part of my movement friends I would have regained strength to come back fighting. But that is exactly what I did not experience.

I was sick and few visited me, hardly anyone from my family, my academic and my movement friends. What was worse was that I didn't even expect them to, so low was my sense of self worth. If it wasn't for the love of a husband who stood by me and provided for me, a husband who learned how to love growing up in a missionary family, I think I would have gone stark-raving mad.

As it was, from the long hours of solitude and virtual solitary confinement, I lost much of my ability to communicate and much of my sense of perspective. I became so inwardly focused that I had difficulty expressing myself outwardly in any way, especially by writing, the skill which was so critical to my sense of self worth as an intellectual. Even speaking became, in unfamiliar company, halting and hesitant.

I eventually regained my health enough to resume graduate studies at U.C. Berkeley in California, where by husband and I now live. I hoped to restore my lost sense of self confidence by pursuing an academic subject in which I had always excelled, the study of ancient languages. I did succeed in proving to myself that I could compete on intellectual terms, for I was an outstanding student in cuneiform studies. But after two years of constant study it soon became apparent that the academic game was all too much like the games I encountered elsewhere—the race was not to the swift. I only ended up more embittered and disillusioned, lost in a morass of self-pity. The Biblical tradition seemingly meant little to me anymore, for I had despaired of any meaning in life. But somehow deep down inside I still cared, I really cared.

It was in my darkest hour, in the moment of deepest despair, that faith began to well up in me like a bubbling spring. In the midst of my greatest awareness of the tragedy of the human condition, the inevitability of human sin, I began, miraculously, to hope. For through years of suffering I was finally learning to put my trust in God alone. I realized now how I had laid expectations on others that only a transcendent God could fulfill. I saw clearly for the first time that the gospel message is the final solution to the human dilemma, the only real answer to the agonizing question: why is truth so often on the scaffold and wrong so often on the throne? In Christ I saw embodied the suffering love which does not succeed on worldly terms (cross) but is nonetheless victorious (resurrection), the paradox which is beyond all human understanding.

Then I learned to pray, learned from a group of radical–counter-culture evangelical Christians (CWLF—Christian World Liberation Front) to whom I turned with a sense of compelling urgency that I can only see as directed by God. The prayer I uttered was the first in my life in which I turned to God in true repentance and acknowledged His/Her sovereignty over my life, and, in effect, surrendered. What I experienced in the "hour I first believed" can only be described as "amazing grace," as a mighty onrush of love, as God's unconditional acceptance.

Paul Tillich put it so well:

> You are accepted. You are accepted, accepted by that which is greater than you. . . . The grace of being able to look frankly into the eyes of another. The miraculous grace of reunion of life with life . . . the power to say yes to ourselves, . . . peace enters into us and makes us whole. . . . self hate and self contempt disappears and . . . oneself is united with itself.

Then began the slow agonizing death of the old self, the long inner struggle which will never in this lifetime be fully over. Coming to know Christ can be likened to culture shock when all the old ego-props are knocked down and the rug literally pulled out from under one's feet. A maturing relationship with God involves the pain of continual self-confrontation as well as the joy of self-fulfillment, a continual dying and rising again, a continual rebirth, the dialectic of judgement and grace. For the first time in my life I have begun to have the strength to face myself as I am, without excuse but equally important, without guilt. I know that I am sinful but I could not bear this knowledge if I did not also know that I am accepted.

I now understand the profundity of I Corinthians 13 when Paul says that all that ultimately matters is love. Human endeavor without it is a "noisy gong or clanging cymbal". One may have "prophetic powers" (i.e. be a perceptive theologian), "understand all mysteries and all knowledge" (i.e. be an insightful intellectual), "give away" all one has or "deliver" one's "body to be burned" (i.e. be a dedicated revolutionary), "have all faith, enough to move mountains" (i.e. be an inspiring preacher), but without love it is nothing, absolutely nothing.

One of the weaknesses of Marxist thinking is that love is not central to it. I have always treasured Che Guevara's words, "At the risk of seeming ridiculous, let me say that a true revolutionary must be guided by great feelings of love." But why is it that he almost had to apologize?

"He who does not know love does not know God, for God is love." That sums it all up for me. Loving care for each other, real sensitivity to each other's needs, is the mark of true Christians, not right doctrine, right ritual, right moral conduct, right emotional expression of spiritual gifts, etc. etc. etc.

What is love? This is not a trivial question given the increasingly common misuse of the word to mean an euphoric high, a high which enables one blissfully to escape rather than painfully to confront the hassles of life. I can best share what I've learned by elucidating Paul's advice, in light of my own experience. "Love is patient and kind," that is, love accepts others where they're at, it allows them to grow at their own rate, though insisting that they grow. "Love is not jealous or boastful," that is, love does not allow ego-tripping but rebukes others in a way that does not put them down. "Love is not arrogant or rude," that is, love does not engage in games of ego-projection and one-upmanship, but rather seeks to draw others out. "Love does not insist on its own way," that is, love does not lay ideological trips on others, including evangelical trips. "It is not irritable or resentful," that is, love does not wallow in bitterness or self-pity, does not waste emotional energy mulling over the ways one has been hurt by others—a hard lesson for me to learn. "It does not rejoice at wrong but rejoices in the right," that is, given all the above, love nonetheless persists in arguing for what is right, boldly expressing its point of view though listening to that of others. Love of another is never an excuse not to be honest.

In my own experience the high ethical ideal of the Scriptures, "to love thy neighbor as thyself," was totally out of the range of possibility until I turned toward God. Without knowing that ultimate acceptance which can only come from God I was trapped in ego-defensiveness, caring only for those who had something to offer me. But as Jesus said:

> Love your neighbor and pray for those who persecute you . . . (Matt. 5:44). For if you love those who love you, what reward have you? Do not even the tax collectors do the same? (Matt. 5:47)

God sensitizes our hearts so that we can take the risk of loving without expecting reciprocation—a very painful but ultimately fulfilling process, a process whereby the self truly dies to be born anew.

It is this strength to hang on despite the cost, despite the odds, the strength that can only come from faith, that is sending me back into the fray fighting. I know now that the struggle to humanize the world, the revolution, is a continual process without final resolution until that day when God acts decisively to pull it all together. But as a Christian I can participate in that struggle without succumbing either to despair or to a false optimism. I can have a realism without cynicism and a hope without illusion.

I know that I will always be one of Jesus' zealot disciples, with the disciples' question at the ascension forever on my lips: "Now Lord will you finally deliver the power to the people?" I will always walk the delicate tightrope between an idolatrous tendency to absolutize revolution and a pietistic copout. But it is on that kind of razor's edge that a Christian must always stand, living in the tension of being "in the world but not of it" (pp. 18–20).

Pamphlets and Promotional Literature

I have used as primary sources the following brochures (mostly undated) from the organizations indicated:

American Scientific Affiliation—"American Scientific Affiliation."

The Billy Graham Center at Wheaton College—"The Billy Graham Center at Wheaton College."

Campus Crusade for Christ International—"The Adventure of Your Life."

Christian Business Men's Committee—"Why CBMC."

Evangelicals Concerned—"Evangelicals Concerned."

Evangelical Theological Society—"The Evangelical Theological Society."

The Fellowship of Witness—"The Fellowship of Witness."

Fuller Theological Seminary—"Fuller Theological Seminary: Facts as of November 1976."

Institute for Christian Studies—"Graduate Study, Institute for Christian Studies, Toronto."

International Fellowship of Evangelical Students—"International Fellowship of Evangelical Students."

Inter-Varsity Christian Fellowship—"Declaring Jesus Christ to This Generation"; "10 Perspectives on Inter-Varsity."

National Association of Evangelicals—"NAE: The Story of Evangelical Cooperation."

National Black Evangelical Association—"Program: National Black Evangelical Association 14th Annual Convention April 13–17, 1977."

Presbyterian Lay Committee—"Questions and Answers: The Presbyterian Lay
    Committee, Inc."; "What You Should Know About the Presbyterian Lay
    Committee."
Presbyterians United for Biblical Concerns—"Presbyterians United for Biblical
    Concerns: An Invitation to Membership" (1975).
The Robert H. Schuller Institute for Successful Church Leadership—"The
    Robert H. Schuller Institute for Successful Church Leadership."
The Theological Students Fellowship—"TSF: Introducing The Theological
    Students Fellowship."
The Other Side—"Jubilee Crafts"; "Jubilee Fund."
The Young Life Campaign—"Affirmation about Young Life"; "Make It Hap-
    pen Here: What Is Urban Young Life?"; "A Report on Young Life's 35th
    Year from Bill Starr, President"; "Young Life's Purpose in Relation-
    ships."
Youth for Christ International—"Internship: A Dialogue"; "Youth for Christ
    Overseas."
Youth Specialties—"Youth Specialties."

Notes

CHAPTER 1

1. "Half of U.S. Protestants Are 'Born Again' Christians," *The Gallup Poll* (September 26, 1976), pp. 1–7.
2. George Gallup, Jr., "U.S. in Early Stage of Religious Revival?" *Journal of Current Social Issues* (Spring 1977), pp. 50–52.

CHAPTER 2

1. Niebuhr, *Christ and Culture,* pp. 32–38.
2. Marty, *A Nation of Behavers,* p. 18.
3. Amitai Etzioni, "The Family: Is It Obsolete?" *Journal of Current Social Issues* (Winter 1977), pp. 4, 5.
4. "Half of U.S. Protestants Are 'Born Again' Christians," *The Gallup Poll* (September 26, 1976), p. 2.
5. See John P. Newport, "Secularization, Secularism, and Christianity," *Review and Expositor* (Winter 1971), pp. 81–93.
6. Marty, *A Nation of Behavers,* p. 37 (the definition comes from Philip Bagby).
7. Quebedeaux, *The Young Evangelicals,* pp. 28–37.

CHAPTER 3

1. Francis A. Schaeffer, *No Final Conflict,* p. 48.
2. Dallas Theological Seminary, *Catalog for 1976–77,* p. 41.
3. Dallas *Catalog,* p. 9.
4. Trinity Evangelical Divinity School, *Catalog for 1975–77,* inside front cover.

5. Henry, *Evangelicals in Search of Identity,* p. 94.
6. Henry, *Evangelicals,* p. 50.
7. See Bernard Ramm, "Carl Henry's Magnum Opus," *Eternity* (March 1977), pp. 58, 59, 61–63.

CHAPTER 4

1. Constant H. Jacquet, Jr., ed., *Yearbook of American and Canadian Churches 1976* (Nashville, Tenn.: Abingdon, 1976), p. 96.
2. Frank S. Mead, *Handbook of Denominations in the United States,* 6th ed. pp. 41–43.
3. Henry, *Evangelicals in Search of Identity,* p. 42.
4. Jacquet, *Yearbook,* p. 71.
5. Mead, *Handbook,* pp. 174–176.
6. See James E. Adams, *Preus of Missouri*.
7. See Donald W. Dayton, *Discovering an Evangelical Heritage*.
8. On denominational particulars, see the relevant articles in Mead, *Handbook*.

CHAPTER 5

1. See "Watergate," *Christianity Today* (January 4, 1974), pp. 8–10, 12–14, 16, 18, 19. In this historic interview, Billy Graham speaks his mind on Watergate and Richard Nixon.
2. On this exposé, see the April 1976 issue of *Sojourners*.
3. "Have You Heard of the Four Spiritual Laws?" (Arrowhead Springs, San Bernardino, Calif.: Campus Crusade for Christ International, 1965).
4. "Before You Give . . . ," *Eternity* (March 1977), pp. 15, 40.
5. "'Here's Life, America!' Campaign Analyzed," *Eternity* (May 1977), pp. 8, 10.
6. Edward E. Plowman, "The View from Lausanne," *Christianity Today* (August 16, 1974), pp. 35–37; and Harold Lindsell, "Lausanne 74: An Appraisal," *Christianity Today* (September 13, 1974), pp. 21, 22, 25, 26.
7. "The Lausanne Covenant" (Minneapolis: Billy Graham Evangelistic Association, 1974). See also the "official" record of the Congress: J.D. Douglas, ed., *Let the Earth Hear His Voice* (Minneapolis: World Wide Publications, 1974).
8. James D. Kennedy, "The Coral Ridge Strategy," Part I, *Christianity Today* (July 28, 1972), pp. 31, 32; and Part II, *Christianity Today* (August 25, 1972), pp. 36, 39. See also Russell Chandler, *The Kennedy Explosion* (Elgin, Ill.: David C. Cook, 1972).

9. C. Peter Wagner, *Church Growth Beyond the Melting Pot* (Atlanta: John Knox Press, 1978), pp. 10–12 (prepublication manuscript).

10. See, for instance, Browne Barr, "Finding the Good at Garden Grove," *The Christian Century* (May 4, 1977), pp. 424–427.

11. Scott Hessek, "Christians and the Supermedia," *Christian Life* (January 1977), pp. 16, 17, 75–79.

CHAPTER 6

1. "Hotel Del Coronado—That's Some Kind of Place!" *CBMC Report* (December 1976), p. 8.

2. See "'Police Honor Night' Big Success for CBMC of Greater Los Angeles," *CBMC Report* (December 1976), pp. 4, 5.

3. Edward E. Plowman, "Bill Gothard's Institute," *Christianity Today* (May 25, 1973), pp. 44, 45. See also Wilfred Bockelman, *Gothard: The Man and His Ministry*.

4. Barrie Doyle, "Super Goals," *Christianity Today* (January 5, 1973), pp. 50, 51; and Watson Spoelstra, "Out of the Huddle, Onto the Field," *Christianity Today* (March 14, 1975), pp. 54, 55.

5. Robert J. Levin and Amy Levin, "Sexual Pleasure: The Surprising Preferences in 100,000 Women," *Redbook* (September 1975), p. 53.

CHAPTER 7

1. See Dayton, *Discovering an Evangelical Heritage*.

2. For the text of the Chicago Declaration and commentary, see Ronald J. Sider, ed., *The Chicago Declaration*.

3. James S. Hewett, "Fuller Graduates," *Theology, News and Notes* (special issue 1976), p. 17.

4. *Seminex Catalog of Courses 1976–77*, p. 20.

5. *Gordon-Conwell Theological Seminary Catalog 1976–77*, p. 21.

6. *Asbury Theological Seminary Bulletin 1976–77*, p. 123.

7. Asbury *Bulletin*, pp. 11, 12.

8. "Where Now Young Evangelicals?" *The Other Side* (March–April 1975), p. 34.

9. *Bulletin of Wheaton College 1977–78*, p. 5.

10. Bruce Larson, "What Makes Theology Relational?" *Faith at Work* (June 1977), pp. 5, 6, 29 (reprinted from *The Relational Revolution* and *Ask Me to Dance*).

11. See Quebedeaux, *The New Charismatics*, pp. 107–143.

12. On the trend toward neo-orthodoxy at Fuller Seminary, see Gerald T. Sheppard, "Biblical Hermeneutics: The Academic Language of Evangelical Identity," *Union Seminary Quarterly Review* (Winter 1977), pp. 81–94.

CHAPTER 8

1. "Christian Organizations Upgrade Standards," *Eternity* (June 1977), pp. 6, 7.
2. Francis A. Schaeffer, *The God Who Is There*, p. 163. On his apologetics, see Thomas V. Morris, *Francis Schaeffer's Apologetics: A Critique*.
3. James Hefley and Marti Hefley, *The Church That Takes on Trouble*.
4. Hefley and Hefley, pp. 136, 137.
5. "Before You Give . . .," *Eternity* (March 1977), p. 40.
6. Stephen Knapp, "Critique of Miguez, Gutierrez: Pivotal Works," *Sojourners* (September 1976), p. 33.
7. See "Interview with Samuel Escobar," *Sojourners* (September 1976), pp. 15–18.
8. See Harold B. Kuhn, "The Evangelical's Duty to the Latin American Poor," *Christianity Today* (February 4, 1977), pp. 67, 68; and the response from Latin American evangelicals, "Today's Oppressed: True 'Exodus' Heirs," *Christianity Today* (June 3, 1977), pp. 23, 24.
9. Carol Kuykendall, "Gene Thomas Touches Lives," *Camera* (Boulder, Colo.), Focus section (December 12, 1976).

CHAPTER 9

1. Russell Chandler, "Ph.D. Scrounges for a Living," *Los Angeles Times* (3) December 1, 1975
2. Walter Hearn, "A Journey Toward Simplicity," *Rādix* (March–April 1977), pp. 11, 16, 17.
3. V. Elving Anderson, "Evangelicals and Science: Fifty Years After the Scopes Trial," in *The Evangelicals* (revised edition), ed. David F. Wells and John D. Woodbridge, pp. 272–274.
4. Ina J. Kau, "Feminists in the American Evangelical Movement" (Unpublished M.A. thesis, Pacific School of Religion, Berkeley, California, 1977), pp. 4, 5. I have used this work as the primary source for my treatment of evangelical feminism.
5. Kau, pp. 16, 17.
6. Kau, pp. 90–95.

7. See Quebedeaux, *The Young Evangelicals,* pp. 109–114.

8. Kau, p. 67.

9. Kau, pp. 108, 109.

10. Kau, p. 111.

11. Kau, p. 107, 108.

12. LaHaye and LaHaye, The Act of Marriage, p. 246.

13. Ralph Blair, ''An Evangelical Look at Homosexuality'' (New York: Homosexual Community Counseling Center, 1972), pp. 2, 3.

CHAPTER 10

1. Marty, *A Nation of Behavers,* p. 70.

2. Marty, p. 71.

3. Unpublished lecture outline, ''Authority in the Church,'' distributed by John C. Bennett in February 1977. All quotes are taken from this outline.

4. ''Confessing Christ Today,'' in *Breaking Barriers: Nairobi* 1975, ed. David M. Paton, pp. 44, 45. The whole text, with an introduction, is on pp. 41–57.

5. See ''A Dialogue with Harvey Cox,'' *Right On* (June 1975), pp. 1, 4, 6, 8, 11.

6. For the text of the appeal, the commentary, see Peter L. Berger and Richard John Neuhaus, eds., *Against the World The Hartford Appeal and the Future of American Religion.*

CHAPTER 11

1. ''Half of U.S. Protestants Are 'Born Again' Christians,'' *The Gallup Poll* (September 26, 1976), p. 1.

2. *Evangelical Newsletter* (December 3, 1976), p. 1.

3. Gish, *The New Left and Christian Radicalism,* p. 42.

4. On the history and development of CWLF, see Donald Heinz, ''Jesus in Berkeley'' (Unpublished Ph.D. dissertation, Graduate Theological Union, Berkeley, California, 1976).

5. Henry, *Evangelicals in Search of Identity,* p. 64.

6. John Wesley, ''The Character of a Methodist'' (Wilmore, Ky.: Good News, n.d.).

7. William F. Bentley, ''Bible Believers in the Black Community,'' *The Evangelicals* (revised edition), ed. David F. Wells and John D. Woodbridge, pp. 128–141.

8. See *The Other Side* (July–August 1975), an issue devoted to the new black evangelicals.

9. John R. W. Stott, ed., *Christ the Liberator,* p. 194.

10. On Skinner, see Quebedeaux, *The Young Evangelicals,* pp. 115–118.

11. "Agenda for the Church: 1976–2000," *Eternity* (January 1976), pp. 15–17, 59–62.

12. See Kenneth L. Woodward, "Roots for Evangelicals," *Newsweek* (May 23, 1977), p. 76.

13. "The Chicago Call: An Appeal to Evangelicals," (Westchester, Ill.: Cornerstone Press, 1977), p. 3.

14. I introduced this typology in "The Evangelicals: New Trends and New Tensions," *Christianity and Crisis* (September 20, 1976), pp. 197–202. Since then it has been further developed by Richard Tholin and Lane T. Dennis, "Radical Evangelicals: Challenge to Liberals and Conservatives," *explor* (Fall 1976), pp. 43–54; and I have used their insights in dealing with the subgroups of the evangelical left.

15. "Yeshua Is the Messiah!" *Time* (July 4, 1977), p. 76. See also Donald R. LaMagdeleine, "Jews for Jesus: Organizational Structure and Supporters" (Unpublished M.A. thesis, Graduate Theological Union, Berkeley, California, 1977), the first careful survey of the organization.

CHAPTER 12

1. Review of Quebedeaux, *The Young Evangelicals,* in *Anglican Theological Review* (July 1975), pp. 380, 381.

Selected Bibliography

Adams, James E. *Preus of Missouri*. New York: Harper & Row, 1977.

Anderson, John B. *Vision and Betrayal in America*. Waco, Texas: Word Books, 1975.

Barth, Karl. *The Epistle to the Romans*. London: Oxford University Press, 1933.

Bass, Clarence. *Backgrounds to Dispensationalism*. Grand Rapids, Mich.: Baker Book House, 1977 (1960).

Bennett, John C. *The Radical Imperative*. Philadelphia: Westminster, 1975.

Benson, Dan. *The Total Man*. Wheaton, Ill.: Tyndale House, 1977.

Berger, Peter, and Richard J. Neuhaus, eds. *Against the World for the World: The Hartford Appeal and the Future of American Religion*. New York: Seabury, 1976.

Bockelman, Wilfred. *Gothard: The Man and His Ministry*. Milford, Mich.: Mott Media, 1976.

Brown, Dale. *The Christian Revolutionary*. Grand Rapids, Mich.: Eerdmans, 1971.

Bube, Richard H. *The Human Quest: A New Look at Science and Christian Faith*. Waco, Texas: Word Books, 1971.

Christenson, Larry. *The Christian Family*. Minneapolis: Bethany Fellowship, 1970.

Clouse, Robert G., Robert D. Linder, and Richard V. Pierard, eds. *The Cross and the Flag*. Carol Stream, Ill.: Creation House, 1972.

Costas, Orlando. *The Church and Its Mission: A Shattering Critique from the Third World*. Wheaton, Ill.: Tyndale House, 1974.

Cox, Harvey. *The Secular City,* revised edition. New York: Macmillan, 1966.

Dayton, Donald W. *Discovering an Evangelican Heritage*. New York: Harper & Row, 1976.

Dennis, Lane T. *A Reason for Hope*. Old Tappan, N.J.: Revell, 1976.

Elliot, Elisabeth. *Let Me Be a Woman*. Wheaton, Ill.: Tyndale House, 1976.

Gish, Arthur G. *The New Left and Christian Radicalism*. Grand Rapids, Mich.: Eerdmans, 1970.

Glickman, S. Craig. *A Song for Lovers*. Downers Grove, Ill.: InterVarsity Press, 1976.

Gutierrez, Gustavo. *A Theology of Liberation*. Maryknoll, N.Y.: Orbis Books, 1972.

Hatfield, Mark. *Between a Rock and a Hard Place*. Waco, Texas: Word Books, 1976.

Hefley, James, and Marti Hefley. *The Church that Takes on Trouble*. Elgin, Ill.: David C. Cook, 1976.

Henry, Carl F. H. *Evangelicals in Search of Identity*. Waco, Texas: Word Books, 1976.

———. *God, Revelation and Authority,* 2 vols. Waco, Texas: Word Books, 1976.

Henry, Paul B. *Politics for Evangelicals*. Valley Forge, Pa.: Judson Press, 1974.

Jewett, Paul K. *Man as Male and Female*. Grand Rapids, Mich.: Eerdmans, 1975.

Kelley, Dean M. *Why Conservative Churches Are Growing,* revised edition. New York: Harper & Row, 1977.

Kennedy, James D. *Evangelism Explosion*. Wheaton, Ill.: Tyndale House, 1970.

LaHaye, Tim, and Beverly LaHaye. *The Act of Marriage*. Grand Rapids, Mich.: Zondervan, 1976.

Larson, Bruce. *Ask Me to Dance*. Waco, Texas: Word Books, 1972.

———. *The Relational Revolution*. Waco, Texas: Word Books, 1976.

Lindsell, Harold. *The Battle for the Bible*. Grand Rapids, Mich.: Zondervan, 1976.

Martin, Walter R. *The Kingdom of the Cults*. Grand Rapids, Mich.: Zondervan, 1965.

Marty, Martin E. *A Nation of Behavers*. Chicago: The University of Chicago Press, 1976.

Mead, Frank S. *Handbook of Denominations in the United States,* 6th edition. Nashville, Tenn.: Abingdon, 1975.

Mollenkott, Virginia Ramey. *Women, Men and the Bible*. Nashville, Tenn.: Abingdon, 1977.

Monsma, Stephen. *The Unraveling of America*. Downers Grove, Ill.: InterVarsity Press, 1974.

Mooneyham, W. Stanley. *What Do You Say to a Hungry World?* Waco, Texas: Word Books, 1975.

Morgan, Marabel. *The Total Woman*. Old Tappan, N.J.: Spire Books, 1975.

———. *Total Joy*. Old Tappan, New Jersey: Revell, 1976.

Morris, Thomas V. *Francis Schaeffer's Apologetics: A Critique*. Chicago: Moody Press, 1976.

Mouw, Richard. *Politics and the Biblical Drama*. Grand Rapids, Mich.: Eerdmans, 1976.

Niebuhr, H. Richard. *Christ and Culture*. New York: Harper & Row, 1951.

Pannell, Bill. *My Friend the Enemy*. Waco, Texas: Word Books, 1968.

Paton, David M., ed. *Breaking Barriers: Nairobi 1975*. Grand Rapids, Mich.: Eerdmans, 1976.

Perkins, John. *Let Justice Roll Down*. Glendale, Calif.: Regal Books, 1976.

———. *A Quiet Revolution*. Waco, Texas: Word Books, 1977.

Quebedeaux, Richard. *The New Charismatics: The Origins, Development, and Significance of Neo-Pentecostalism*. Garden City, N.Y.: Doubleday, 1976.

———. *The Young Evangelicals*. New York: Harper & Row, 1974.

Robinson, John A. T. *Honest to God*. Philadelphia: Westminster, 1963.

———. *Redating the New Testament*. Philadelphia: Westminster, 1976.

Rogers, Jack, ed. *Biblical Authority*. Waco, Texas: Word Books, 1977.

Scanzoni, Letha, and Nancy Hardesty. *All We're Meant to Be: A Biblical Approach to Women's Liberation*. Waco, Texas: Word Books, 1974.

Schaeffer, Francis A. *Escape from Reason*. Downers Grove, Ill.: InterVarsity Press, 1968.

——— *The God Who Is There*. Downers Grove, Ill.: InterVarsity Press, 1968.

———. *No Final Conflict*. Downers Grove, Ill.: InterVarsity Press, 1975.

Sider, Ronald J., ed. *The Chicago Declaration*. Carol Stream, Ill.: Creation House, 1974.

Sider, Ronald J. *Rich Christians in an Age of Hunger*. Downers Grove, Ill.: InterVarsity Press, 1977.

Skinner, Tom. *If Christ Is the Answer, What Are the Questions?* Grand Rapids, Mich.: Zondervan, 1974.

Smedes, Lewis B. *Sex for Christians*. Grand Rapids, Mich.: Eerdmans, 1976.

Snyder, Howard K. *The Problem of Wineskins: Church Structure in a Technological Age*. Downers Grove, Ill.: InterVarsity Press, 1975.

Stott, John R.W., ed. *Christ the Liberator*. Downers Grove, Ill.: InterVarsity Press, 1971.

Wallis, Jim. *Agenda for Biblical People*. New York: Harper & Row, 1976.

Wheat, Ed, and Gaye Wheat. *Intended for Pleasure*. Old Tappan, N.J.: Revell, 1977.

Wells, David F., and John D. Woodbridge, eds. *The Evangelicals,* revised edition. Grand Rapids, Mich.: Baker Book House, 1977.

Yoder, John H. *The Politics of Jesus*. Grand Rapids, Mich.: Eerdmans, 1972.

Index